During the 30 years Miriam Pederson and I were colleagues, she shared her remarkable gift of bringing out talent in young writers with patience, skill, and mastery. At the same time, I was gifted by her remarkable talent as a poet in her own right at readings, in writing groups, and writing conferences where we taught together.

Miriam is a brilliant poet of the everyday. She writes of childhood (hers and her children's), of parents and parenting, of ordinary objects being used and at rest. Subtly, her poetry reveals surprising depths beneath the surfaces of things. She draws the outer world exquisitely, without a wasted word, with lean, elegant phrasing, then reveals a mostly benevolent, sometimes mysterious, and personally felt divinity lurking just below the surface. Miriam's poetry does what all good poetry is meant to do—it changes the way we move through the world. Those who knew her will hear her voice in every line of this collection; those who did not know her will find a friend they never knew they had.

—Gary Eberle
Professor of English, emeritus, Aquinas College
Author of *Angel Strings, Sacred Time and the Search for Meaning,* and
Dangerous Words: Talking about God in an Age of Fundamentalism

Throughout her life, Miriam Pederson was an extraordinary teacher, mentor, colleague and friend. In this, her posthumous collection of over 300 poems (many of which have never been published before), she shines as a unique and gifted poet. Spanning several decades of her rich and creative life, *All Fine in the Floating World: The Collected Poetry of Miriam Pederson*, reflects a wide range of subjects and themes about faith, nature, community and friends, marriage and children, sleep and dreams, longing and loss, hope, and so much more. These poems are filled with pure, unadorned grace and honest, clear-eyed wisdom. With a simple yet elegant style, she takes life's ordinary moments and weaves them into luminescent images that have a haunting familiarity: in essence, she gives us our lives. Her language is natural and perfectly paced as it embraces joy and sorrow with equal and delicate measure. The last line of the last poem in the book, "What is Our Deepest Desire?", shares that embrace with us as the narrator ponders death and "...the way to enter and leave this world." It is a poignant and brilliant witness to a remarkable legacy, a remarkable life.

—Linda Nemec Foster
Author of *Bone Country* and *The Blue Divide*
Past Poet Laureate of Grand Rapids, Michigan

All Fine in the Floating World: The Collected Poetry of Miriam Pederson is ideally titled. Despite arthritis, which brought many trials to her adult life, and in her final months, a stubborn foot infection, which confined Miriam to the house, her spirit rose above her physical plights. Rarely, if ever did she bring them up in conversation and only when asked. Infrequently her poetry dealt with the inflammation of her joints and their limitations, but when it did, as in "When the Hand Loses Its Music" it was a special poem, in this case winning the Kent County Poetry Contest in 1984. She faced her afflictions with determination and humor: "Your ruined fist / gapes like an empty purse," or "Even as your outstretched hand / is misread / as a signal to stop everything."

Because Miriam devoted her life to faith and transcendence, her poems seem even more vital. They filter into an opening section which begins with "Faith," and long middle section comprised of numerous headings, and an ending category entitled "Hope." Miriam's poems are a testament to her courage as much as her finesse with language and her will to stake out her own path and not be detoured on her road through life. This collection is a celebration of who Miriam was and continues to be through this living, breathing volume.

Rodney Torreson
Author of *The Ascension of Sandy's Drive-In*
Past Poet Laureate of Grand Rapids, Michigan

a POuEM for
MrS. Miriam

MrS. Miriam Like a gentle wave of kindness She is, Like a Leaf gently blowing in the wind with A trail of other Leaves folowing her, family and feinds.

from: Hope

All Fine in the Floating World

All Fine in the Floating World

The Collected Poetry

of Miriam Pederson

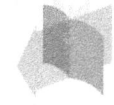

Chapbook Press

Schuler Books
2660 28th Street SE
Grand Rapids, MI 49512
(616) 942-7330
www.schulerbooks.com

ISBN 13: 9781957169699

Library of Congress Control Number: 2023922189

All Fine in the Floating World:
The Collected Poetry of Miriam Pederson

Printed in the United States by Chapbook Press.

Production Team
Joyce Alene Recker (editor), Mara Naselli (copy editor),
Amy Dunham Strand, Pamela Dail Whiting
Cover Design / Photograph: Dana Freeman
Sculpture, *All Fine in the Floating World:* Ron Pederson
Hope Lorenz, *A Powem for Mrs. Miriam*

This collection of poetry is in celebration
of Miriam Pederson's life and poetry

and is dedicated with love
to her family—

Ron

Ben

Madeline and Luke
and their children,
Clara and Oscar

CONTENTS

INTRODUCTION

Poetry was intrinsic to every dimension of Miriam Pederson's life. She was a brilliant ambassador for poetry—a public poet who participated in formal poetry events, led workshops, taught in the schools, gave readings, served on fine arts boards and committees, and exhibited broadsides together with her husband, sculptor Ron Pederson. Miriam wove poetry into everyday experience and relationships. Always curious and empathetic, Miriam encircled life and people through poetry, with perceptive mirth, intelligence, and appreciation. Often shared over wine, tea, or a meal, poetry brought people together and built community. For Miriam, poetry was communion and prayer, through which she honored both the human spirit and the Mystery in the ordinary.

Through *writing* poetry, Miriam communed with the spiritual heart. Miriam wrote some poems in conversation with art, especially Ron's sculptures, like the one featured on the cover of this collection, where poetry and art embrace one another. Some of Miriam's more abstract and exceptional poems, like "The Seller of Birds" series, came from just such a dance with art. Yet most of Miriam's poems emerged from lived experience—from braiding a daughter's hair, listening to a husband's snoring, having tea and marmalade with a friend, or pumping water alongside other women. In her poems, ordinary moments are rendered with profound detail in ways that affirm life's goodness without sentimentality or dogma. While the poems read with ease, everything in the poems is intentional, careful, and conscious.

For Miriam, the *reading* of poetry, whether in bookstores, campus coffee shops, English department offices, church meetings, or friends' homes, was also an invitation to gather. Miriam regularly read and discussed poems with friends, together relishing a common love of language. In these conversations, Miriam always contributed further perspective about the poem's context or form, or the poet's background, or maybe she had met or hosted the poet. Her poetry friends leaned into her intimate knowledge and into her creation of kinship through poetry. This collection grew out of these gatherings.

Miriam thought poems should be necessary—that they not rest in stylistic maneuvers but say something from one heart to another and call us to our humanity. She appreciated what she called poems of heft—poems that are not obtuse or needlessly difficult, but that carry spiritual depth and show us the world and its painful beauty. Miriam was also drawn to, and perhaps even required, musicality in poems; she focused on the sound of language. Like her own musical laughter, Miriam's poems carry light and affirmation—a sense of yes—through sound as well as image. Miriam's poetry shows us a *turning toward* the world and toward others. Even when she was in great pain and things were by no means fine for her, her poems courageously create a "fine, floating world" for us.

All Fine in the Floating World aims to honor Miriam's entire life. This volume, in line with her generous spirit, is expansive and eclectic and speaks to her wide-ranging relationships. It is dedicated to her family—her husband Ron, son Ben, daughter Madeline, son-in-law Luke, and her grandchildren, Clara and Oscar. Her family's loving leadership in locating and organizing over fifty years of poems into themes, moving from general observations to personal reflection on Miriam's life and faith, has culminated in a collection reflecting an ongoing dialogue of creative collaborators. At the center of the collection is Miriam's trust in the spiritual, as reflected in the opening and closing sections "Faith" and "Hope" and the prefatory poem "Constants."

Some of the sections in the collection warrant special attention. The series poems, such as "His Life," "The Professor," "Seller of Birds," and "The West of Ireland," were intended as series and have been left intact and separated to preserve their unity. The Ireland poems testify to the Pedersons' connection with the Ireland Program in Tully Cross, where they led Aquinas College students for five semesters. An inscription of one such poem, "We Are Sleeping in Ireland," now accompanies a tree planted in Tully Cross as part of a June 2023 memorial tribute, given on the program's fiftieth reunion. Tully Cross energized Miriam's poetry, and some of her energy will remain with Tully Cross and the people there.

Some of these poems could easily slide from one section of the collection to another, such as the New Year's poems. These are pulled from the Pedersons' tradition of combining art and a poem each new year on a postcard for family and friends, who eagerly anticipated their arrival in the mail and often pinned them on refrigerators or cork boards. These New Year's poems became touchstones, providing spiritual orientation for many throughout the year.

Miriam paid attention to relationships and to daily things—rolling marbles and Scrabble tiles, the eye of a housefly and industry of ants, children's play and contented pets, neighbors' casseroles, wrinkled faces, sheets on a clothesline, fiery peonies, autumn birds, and all the floating stuff of seasons. Her poetry brings together humor and mystery, light and dark, flight and depth, showing us how to live lovingly and well, how to embrace all of life, how to *be* the "Woman on the Sled" who "will not drag her feet." As Miriam sent her poetry into our lives, we celebrate her life in *All Fine in the Floating World: The Collected Poetry of Miriam Pederson.*

Amy Dunham Strand
Dana Freeman
Joyce Alene Recker
Mara Naselli
Pamela Dail Whiting

PRELUDE

CONSTANTS

Faith and hope sustain us
though we run full-tilt
toward an unknown country.
We lift our packs
from our shoulders,
raise our arms in celebration,
gulp precious air, and forget
that victory is fleeting.

I want to believe
my mother's bread bowl,
cracked and chipped, will hold its own
always—
empty for years, but sturdy,
inviting my hands to make a mark
into the soft, pliable dough
of a given day.

FAITH

for an instant, feel that ancient depth of darkness—
its power to make us see
the limits of our knowing

EPIPHANY

A spool of thread drops from the table
and rolls underneath the sofa
joining two marbles, a penny dated 1957,
and a #2 pencil.
Lie down and peer into the dark space
between sofa springs and floor.
When your eyes adjust,
place yourself among the lost and found.
In this humble space you can see
what muscles the heavens with infinite churning,
what calls the dazzle out of the dark,
what etches the night sky with the day of your birth.

DEEPER

He who knows about depth knows about God.
—Paul Tillich

To go deeper is to enter the place we cannot see.
Yet evidence is there—and so we dig
beneath the snow, the frozen grass,
the granite, the basalt, on to the inner core.

Like a magnet we are drawn to know
a place of grace, a place of more,
so deeper we must grow.

I REMEMBER BURNING

As a child in church,
my bare legs varnished to the pew,
I watched the face
of Reverend Fissel
work itself into a sweat
and pant toward a second wind.
Grace and I made paper fans,
fingers deepening the folds.
Our hair would lift and swirl
as we fanned each other, eyes closed.
From the choir loft
mother's glare seared through our lids.
The fans dropped,
withered flowers in our laps,
while the organ bellowed
"Just as I Am."
People rose,
drifted toward the altar,
their shirts clinging to their backs.
They were being saved from the fires of Hell.
By the eighth verse,
Grace would have fallen asleep,
but I never could
for the heat.

A MEMORY

At age eleven, her appendix burst,
doubled over, coiled like a fist.
The doctor, sure that it was something else,
held her hand and took her pulse.
Nine days she lay in a hospital room,
some wondered if she'd ever go home.
The nurses' faces spun around, around,
and something told her she had sinned, had sinned,
and she could feel her parents' blossoming grief,
their prayers cut through her conscience like a knife.
The anesthesia lifted her on wings
and the fluorescence spoke to her in tongues.
When she awoke, she promised to be good;
a thousand other things she promised God.
And when the poison finally seeped away,
the velvet reds of roses caught her eye.
She asked the nurse to brush her tangled hair,
she touched her face, she touched the swollen scar,
she felt her pulse, and counted all her friends,
and thought of summer camp, the smell of pines.
As she rode home, she watched the cloudless sky
and kissed each promise that she'd made to God good-bye.

CLOSE

The nearly beautiful, innocent, or dead among us
are those who linger in our thoughts;
perhaps just changing the angle slightly
will allow them passage, and finally their entrance.
Almost the horseshoe rings the spike,
the competitor wiping his hands on his jeans,
squinting in the August heat.
Whatever brushes against your sleeve
in the dark is a foolish imagining, yet
you stiffen before switching on the light.
Now, ear to the ground, you think you hear
all the horses of heaven approaching,
grass weaving into your hair
in a wind that surely bodes change.

COMMON GROUND

Yours is the wanting,
mine is the holding.
Yours is the seed,
mine is the harvest.
All the talk, talk, talk
piling up like unpaid bills
becomes the dwelling place
in which, finally,
we place our hands on the table
and partake of the bread.

DELIVERANCE

Friends arrive at my door carrying meals.
Nourishment and generosity
waft through my house.
Well wishes nestle around my heart.
But it will not lift—this severing thing called pain.

When I was a child and suffered from ear aches,
I remember the voice of my mother
behind the throb; *oh, sweetheart!*
she would softly say, and I would sob,
please, Mommy, make it go away
—and it did: away from my body,
away from my bedroom, away from my life.

Now when my imploring, ever so fervent,
falls short of the hearing of the One
whose healing garment eludes me,
I wrestle with my old belief
here in this place of no deliverance,
but like the lost sheep pulled from the tangle,
or the melody that lifts you out of yourself
and sets you down gently at the door of another,
I will be salvaged by the chicken casseroles,
the homemade bread, and fresh tomatoes
brought by these holy messengers
sent to assure me I am not forsaken.

GOD CREATED ALABASTER

Invisible lines scored the world
before brooks and rivers
ran with water.
As God envisioned the Nile,
the Mississippi, the Thames
on the infant earth,
He found himself composing music.
The trumpet sounded
in what became
the mountains of Tibet
and one by one
the instruments joined
driving the melody
until it burst into rivers.

All the veined things
that God created—
men and women,
leaves and roots,
lightning,
were symphonies once.

But God also created alabaster,
its beautiful impurities
locked in frozen rivers,
the mute stone a prophecy
of hearts hardening
in days to come.

ENTERING

In the slow consciousness of morning,
light enters this room like a luminous hand
touching walls, brushing aside ashes of night,
arranging the furnishings of a new day.
Here is my life, a calm lake, a gentle unfolding.

Under another sky, skin and bone
enter the coughing hunger of dawn.
Someone slices the sun with a weapon
as it rises over the broken procession.

How to square this and that—
the cosmic shrug or the whirlwind of God
condensing the question of justice into
rain falling over all?

CAVES

When men and women drew their hungers and fears
in ochre and plant dyes
on the torch-lit walls of caves,
they believed in the magic of the line
following curves of limestone—
here the belly of a bull, a horse's flying tail,
an arrow hitting home again and again.

One person's sigh was another's there
in the clammy shelter, its journeying echo
transmitting relief, resignation
through hundreds of subterranean chambers.

Some passages lead to the light, some to nowhere
and the blind cave creatures—bats and crickets
know which is which, by the sound, perhaps,
the rhythmic dripping here, not here,
or by the temperature's subtle changes.

Cave tours as we know them
shed colored lights
on all that was unseen before.
The guide, ready to explain the drawings,
the formations, the mysteries,
offers up some entertainment.
But when the moment comes for turning off the lights,
we huddle together, our cameras forgotten.
In the wake of nervous titters,
the rustling of clothing,
we touch the shoulders of our children
and for an instant feel that ancient depth of darkness—
its power to make us see
the limits of our knowing.

LEDGE

The sky holds your trust,
the earth your attention.
Lean forward, step back—
harm is closer than you think.
Fear is a thief,
caution a mother
watching from the porch
as you look both ways.

LISTENING TO ISAIAH

I will not forget you.
See, I have engraved you on the palms of my hands
Isaiah 49: 15, 16

When morning has no promise,
when you hear the slam of doors,
the clicking tongue of disapproval,
when nothing bends or starts or opens,
when you wish for someone's presence
then find it not enough,
when sunlight mocks your losses,
leafy shadows dance against your grief,
when, despite the hunger, taste is bitter,
try to remember who you really are,
your indelible name
engraved in the palms of His hands.

SOLSTICE

Twice in the year, the sun stands still,
and we take note in some nodding, poetic way—
calendar of the ancients, pagan extravaganza,
nothing much to do with this job, my monthly payments.

Seasons enter and exit our neighborhood
lawnmowers, rakes, shovels—implements of removal
to make room for the next onslaught of sprout and wilt.
Is this the cycle we've come to know?

Something remarkable north of the celestial equator
has occurred, steady and predictable as hunger and thirst—
a lingering of light, and extra measure of radiance
ushering in the season we're always waiting for.

If we could stand with Joshua, that Old Testament strategist,
his prayer answered for a stationary sun,
we too would celebrate this yearly lengthening of day
with the awe of the ancients:
something beyond a point of ecliptic intersection,
beyond the science we can name.
A miracle, we'll call it, to allow for savoring
the rich fabric of this day—to admire its weave, its texture,
as it unfurls before us,
drawing us into its generosity of light.

NEXT

Some make the passage with ease,
but you and I, our feet unsure,
inch forward.
In our element,
we see the earth up close:
elders with no time to lose.
Ears to the ground,
we learn what comes next.

NOVEMBER

The brittle and the supple,
the bowed and the swaying,
the blushing and the fading,
the ripe and the hollow,
the broken and the whole,
the shimmering and the bruised,
the bent and the standing,
the hovering and the resting,
the golden and the copper,
the covered and the naked,
the soft and the hardened,
the sweet and the bitter,
the sterile and the fertile,
the chosen and the discarded,
the feathered and the smooth,
the rotted and the sprouting,
the rooted and the scattered,
the fallen and the risen,
the invisible and the impossible.

SEEKER

How long can you go door to door
with your puzzles and question marks,
bearing the day's heavy news on your back?

You are called upon to seek
until you find
to knock until it opens
to decipher the graffiti
of this world.

Your work is cut out for you—
canvassing this barren land
for one small greening—
a color that you'd miss
if you were not so hungry
for its nourishment, its blessing.

INSTRUCTIONS FOR FALLEN ANGELS

Make earth your home,
foolhardy as it is.
Sever the strings that lifted you
above the crowd, above the law.
With your broken wings
you will never again be sublime.
Be human; do some earthly good.

STIRRING

Birds, loud and persistent at 5 a.m.,
silence themselves around 6 to breakfast
on bugs and earthworms before they burst forth
in full-throated song—a call and response
to morning light, drowning out even the mowers,
pathing to and fro in their drone to spring.
Everywhere blossoms bounce nonchalantly,
flaunting their reckless splendor.

All this stirring and reviving
means nothing to those whose bodies are "at rest"—
this state of stillness where grave markers
assure us they are gone from the world
of bees and umbrellas, mail, and all moving things.

I'd like to think the earth rewards all
creatures whose dates have expired.
Nothing is final, even there in the dark
where souls listen for the resurrection
of birdsong from their nesting places.

TRUE BELIEVERS

for Ron and Ben

Above, below
Heaven, earth
Internal, external
Mental, spiritual
Temporal, liminal
Visual, conceptual
Known, unknown
Father, son
Here, there . . .
True believers.

WALKING THE LABYRINTH

As you enter the winding passage,
pattern draws you into an ancient dance,
a sacred game of finding the center.
Unique in gait and posture,
each pilgrim bears a different load:
this one, petitions of a heavy heart;
this one, a snarl of hurt and anger;
another, a stir of curiosity.
Sleeves brush as two travelers pass,
reminder of a journey shared,
a concentric quest.
See how the path turns in on itself
as if to lead you astray,
but with each step,
something old and cumbersome falls away
and you persevere with hope renewed,
with the lightness of letting go.
After you finally enter the place
where rest is waiting—
the heart of the rose,
the palm of God's hand—
you become aware
that though the way back
is the same winding path,
you will be a different traveler
bearing precious gifts
on your return to the world.

WAITING

Someone has promised
its arrival—perhaps in the form
of a circus caravan,
excitement unfurling
throughout the town—
or a zeppelin floating
amidst *ooohs* and *aaahs*
of the faithful.
Possibly it will wend its way
into our own cyber world.

We can only guess
at how it will be manifested,
but for now we will wait,
hope wrapped around us
like Elijah's cloak.

WHAT DO YOU EXPECT

from this solid world?
Some package of happiness
wrapped in foil
to appear steaming on your plate?
A roar of applause
deafening you to the erratic
beat of your heart?
Better to submerge in aquatic stillness
where fishermen's nets float
empty for days,
where emptiness and fullness meet
in the spiraling shell.
Here expectations are weightless bubbles
rising to the surface,
disappearing into thinnest air.

THE PROPHET

Even at a distance you can recognize him.
His gait is odd—stubborn, arhythmic.
His face tilts upward—he is listening to some voice,
watching birds soar and wheel—
he makes some sense of this.
Face to face, he appears less man than scarecrow
propped up by supernatural force.
When his eyes fall into mine, sure of what they see,
I shudder in the pool of his gaze.
My heart pounds as he opens the wings of his mouth.
His words scuttle through my disbelief
like leaves from an ancient tree.

A PRESENCE

It happens as if it has always happened.
A calm settles over you
and your breathing evens out.

The voice that echoed disaster
in your ear, that beckoned your despair,
is strangely silenced.

You are aware of a Presence,
like the hand of your mother on your forehead,
gently easing your fever.

This is what it is to be led
beside still waters, to believe
in this moment
that goodness and mercy will follow you
all the days of your life.

SELECTED NEW YEARS POEMS
2000—2020

Let this new year lift us higher
than what is—to what can be

WISHES FOR YOUR NEW YEAR

A faith to lift you up,
A place to lay your burdens down,
Wisdom to know when to climb
or descend,
Where to mark a new beginning
or graceful end,
A steady boat
as waters rise and fall.

NEWS

In the center of the newspaper
that daily breaks your heart,
cut a hole, and through it
view the comforts of your home,
your loved one's face,
sunlight glancing through the blinds,
calling your attention
to the good news of your life.

GIVEN

News today becomes no news tomorrow.
Gravity holds us up and lets us down.
But light enters day without a glitch,
spreading itself evenly on this earth
as eyes are opened and bodies rise.
What will we do with this common gift
wrapped in heartache and sweetness,
delivered without expectation,
this thing of uncommon grace?

CLEMENTINES

Each dark morning
Our fingers seek their light,
These small suns of winter
Dispelling cold and grey
With tangy bursts
Of momentary joy.

WAKING IN THE NEW YEAR

The shapeless new year
soon will form itself
as we sleep and wake
to stars and morning sun
or darkness deep and
daylight pale as milk.

Together we will rise and enter
our kitchens
where God is perking coffee
and urging us, *It's time!*
Wake up!

CLARA

Nothing is sure
but the stirring of life
buried like a treasure
under layers of doubt.
But look!
A new life comes forth,
a breathing radiance
to hold in our arms.

SKATING THE NEW YEAR

Clear the rink
of the old year,
its sorrows and foibles,
its successful hurrahs.
Scrape away all that obscures
and tie on your skates—
the new ones that fit.
Glide forward and backward
in the grace of knowing
the ice will hold you,
the heavens enfold you.

GRACE

Again the new year comes
with its unpredictable footage:
this time we enter the clearing,
our faces bright with relief . . .
or we stumble into the thicket,
caught helpless for months—
but always the film is running,
the plot unfolding, sun up, sun down,
director cheering us on,
giving us the cues we need to rejoice or mourn,
the grace to be authentic,
the hope for a blockbuster.

GIFTS

What can we do with this day?
Each one enters majestically:
today in glistening white,
soon in browns and delicate greens.
Each holds an offering
priceless as gifts of the Magi.

NEW CALENDAR

A clean slate waits
for notes and reminders.
How will I fill
each perfect, empty square?

God, spread your hand
across each page of days
and I will draw its outline
to intersect my life.

A STRONG HUNCH FOR THE NEW YEAR

If we mind the sky,
the water, our words,
our hearts,
and the way
a loved one turns to face us
in sorrow or in joy,
this year will bring goodness
in the midst of all that is otherwise.

MILLENNIUM

The grand new year
enters our lives
with dazzle and speed.
Together with you
we hold hands
and travel in its starry wake.

INTENTIONS

Your morning coffee
brings the sunrise
and the best intentions.

Intentions stand alert,
obedient disciples
ready to do your will.

Will is a snowdrift
frozen in January,
still and waiting.

Waiting, you learn,
is how grace unfolds—
the sunrise will come,
intentions will do their best.

WEATHER

What stirs in the atmosphere
of this new year—
surprising or predictable—
let it come with the mercy of rain,
the generosity of warmth,
the patience of snow.
Let it come without harm.
Or if it must storm—
let us take shelter
in the Maker of weather
and the care of each other.

RISE

Time to board an air balloon
to rise above the rancor,
the usandthem, the foolishness
of all that is not just
and open hearted.
Let this new year lift us higher
than what is—to what can be.
Our loved ones, passed ones, new ones,
we'll honor with this rising.
The weather is right,
the burners are lit now—
release and make it happen.

HIS LIFE

When he was a youth he had lived his life in a state of the liveliest expectation, thinking to himself: what a fine thing it will be to become a man and to know what to do—like an Apache youth who at the right time goes out into the plains alone, dreams, sees visions, returns, and knows he is a man. But no such time had come and he still didn't know how to live.

—Walker Percy
The Last Gentleman

TIMING

He is the one
whose timing is almost right,
whose glass rises and clinks
a grace note too late,
or whose applause lingers
one clap beyond the audience,
making the performer swallow
before taking the bow.
He may have left
part of his tongue
on the climbing bars
at his grade school years ago
while his classmates, unpunished,
tasted the cold.
Opportunities yawn and fold
all around him
as he sits at some fundraiser
lisping a joke
to his melted parfait.
He tries to compensate,
takes a time management course,
but this timing is in the genes.
The girl, the storm, the stock market
take him by surprise,
and you wonder how in the world
he was born.

SUNDAY MORNINGS

He wades in the marsh near the golf course
gathering misguided balls:
Precept, Strata, Top Flite.
He considers them
in the jubilant din of cicadas and birds,
spreads them on the grass to dry.
As a kid
he cut open a golf ball
and found under its shining hard surface
a maze of elastic string long enough
to reach across the street
to his best friend's house.
Then the hard inner core
he could bounce as high
as the red maple.
He never cared for the sport,
but these dimpled spheres
strangely bless him now,
replenishing their numbers
on the days he goes to work.

DIRECTIONS

He knows the signs:
changes in barometric pressure,
temperament of sky,
direction of the wind.
The almanac guides him,
allows him to think.
Weather penetrates his insular office life,
seeps into his speech
like a foreign dialect,
catches his pen
in an unknown current,
rides on his back
whispering wrong directions,
makes light of his work,
turns him backward toward home.

SHELLS

As he speaks
with his mother on the phone
he imagines her
fingering the shells,
hears them clicking
as she tells him of her day
at the hospital,
of the kindness, the cleanliness.
This night he could not face her
in the antiseptic room.

Her moon snails, pheasant shells,
dove shells, and olives
surround her like a skirt.
She knows them well—
their markings, inner chambers,
on what shore each was found.

Summers long ago
he would walk with her
on the beach in the early morning.
She taught him vigilance,
but lost him somewhere
soon after his childhood.

Her illness brought him back to her.
Now she holds his hand,
turns it over and over
looking for its pattern,
trying to place it.

SPINAL CHORD

In all its dissonance the sound spreads
through tissue, muscle, and nerve,
aching to be resolved—
a cooling harmonic to quiet
cacophony of middle age.

He would give anything
to be the upstanding, upright boy
whistling sweetly toward manhood,
unaware that pain
is but a grace note away.

He learns the broken music well
as the body bends its ear
toward backbone blend of hum and howl,
straining to hear the ring
of mercy's distant chimes.

RESERVATIONS

In college
he would wait for her
on the conservatory steps,
stare at trees,
listen for her touch.
The command of her small hands
astonished him,
piano concertos lifting the leaves
with their energy.
After her practice,
from behind glass doors,
he'd catch sight of her face,
flushed and alive with her gift.

If his eyes could see
the clefs of her mind,
its music welcoming him,
calling him "friend"
in a multitude of languages,
he would cross borders,
carry her on his back if need be.

And she might do the same
if she could be sure
that the steadiness of his gaze
meant more than need,
that the hand enfolding hers
could open with the ease
a flower takes the sun.

MUSIC

His daughter thinks
he doesn't love her.
She watches
from the corner of her eye
as he reads
or opens the refrigerator.
When he's not looking,
she opens the book
he is reading,
hoping to begin a conversation,
but she is afraid it will fail.
Instead,
she practices her clarinet,
speaks to him,
her small room blossoming
with sound.
During the cadenza,
she imagines her head
on his shoulder, his hand taking hers
and gently moving it
nearly in time to the music.

DISPLAYS

He remembers a morning
years ago,
his wife braiding their daughter's hair,
the two sitting on the child's bed.
When he walked past
to say goodbye,
the sun on the frosted window
backlit their figures.
Their hair became two fiery halos,
the solemn faces
turned toward his.

Now his wife
arches over her roses,
reasoning with her too vain daughter
away at school.
He watches her
between articles in *The Journal*,
finds himself envying
her earnest attention,
wonders if beauty
could sustain him this way.

SIGHT

All winter long
he sighs into the walls
of his apartment
feels his wife, daughter,
his work, his house
losing focus.
Reflections from his glasses
splash eyes across the ceiling.
He thinks he sees God
slowly shaking His head.
If spring will come,
he can go north,
lie against the earth
and watch the kettling hawks.
Somewhere he'd read
these birds were guided in migration
by celestial bodies.
He will go north—
test his vision
in a country
radiant with flight.

FROM THE AQUARIUM

The eye
watches him
afloat in the easy chair,
pages turning in the tide.
The man nods
in a maze of fine print.

For a moment
a snail moves between them,
a partial eclipse.

Through artificial sea weed,
over marbles,
the medieval castle,
the eye—
a dark planet—
follows its course.

Now behind the castle
the eye regards the piano
beached on the oriental rug,
the lamp
undulating light,
his wavering shadow.

REMEDIES

He opens the cupboard
trying to recall the names of medicines,
books and exercises,
things recommended.
But this room is a place
where knowing is private—
a trickle of salt across a table,
a glass of cold milk
reflecting the room in his hand.
If he sits in this place
long enough, in the darkness,
he will hear someone far off
stirring ashes,
then sparks from the ancient fire.
Those before him
will gather in the warmth,
cook and eat
and share remedies
for the unnamed illness
he carries room to room.

WEIGHTS

His friends at work
are working out at lunchtime.
So he joins the club,
embarrassed to appear
in his unkempt body,
more embarrassed to go it alone,
pastrami sandwiches at the local deli.
He thinks of all the work
he has before him,
the sweat, the strain
to define himself again.
The Nautilus
reflects his discomfort
as he counts his way back
to the body,
weights lifting him
toward the elemental stuff
that calls itself a man.

RIDE

His bicycle rattles
into the church parking lot
where he cools down
after the uphill sprint.
He circles near the windows
to see the sanctuary,
its white hush easing the burn
of his shoulders and legs.
He no longer feels pain
in his chest
after a strenuous ride
past the old neighborhood,
the grade school of his daughter
now grown and far away.
Once more he circles by the windows
praying for the heart
to ride home.

PAINTING HIS HOUSE

He thinks about those
who gather in circles,
dark faces attentive
to sounds of chainsaws,
trees falling around them
like birds
shot from the sky.

As each ribbon of paint
adheres to the next,
he sees more clearly
his sorrow bound to theirs.

From his ladder
he paints colonial gray.
When he hears drums
or the young deer crackling
on the spit
he doesn't break for iced tea,
but paints until dusk.

THAT SUMMER

Summer began as it always had—
cottonwood seeds drifting in their lazy randomness,
everyone, everything, shedding
while weeds made their break with the earth.

Something was broken in July—
unspent grief pouring out in the heat,
his heavy heart a winter coat
he could not shed or wish away.

In August sorrow settled in his spine.
There was comfort in knowing where it stayed.
Those who loved him waited for the shedding
of his pain, for September's break from summer.

Autumn sheds the ripe and over-ripeness,
pods break open, colors spin and settle on the earth.
His shoulders loosen as he begins a long migration.

TAKING ON THE SEASON

He is raking leaves at midnight,
combing grass beneath the Hunter's moon.
When he gathers armloads for the basket,
leaves escape him.

A leaf pile flares and smokes by a shed,
an aroma so primal
the ache of childhood
creeps around his heart.

In the shaded upstairs window,
he sees his wife's silhouette
illuminated,
an alien or a saint
on the gleaming surface of the house.

He shivers,
but frost beginning its rounds
cannot move him.
He is rooted
like the tree of heaven,
groping at stars
in the night sky.

PRECARIOUS

Leaning closer to hear the song
of the loon,
he senses the imbalance.
How music can displace the world
we know, losing the agenda,
emptying our pockets of purpose.
Soon a gong will send him overboard
into a long decay of sound.
With awkward, happy strokes
he will swim toward home.

THE TRAIN

He's been reading this novel for months.
Before sleep the same passage,
urgent and steady
as the cicada.
This is not the turning point
of the story
but a moment
in the life of the boy,
running,
trying to keep pace with a train.
He thinks he can run this fast
and for a few seconds,
before the train builds its speed,
he does.
Small legs and enormous faith
blaze through the ravine
like grass fire.
These are things he wants to think about.

FOREST

Color has drawn him into the maze
of the Hiawatha Forest.
It is hunting season,
but he doesn't know it yet.
Maple leaves tick
as they touch the forest floor,
a roar is in the oaks
whose fullness speaks to him
of hanging on despite the wind,
despite the song of letting go.
Past the hardwoods
and into the evergreen mass he forges.
Gun shots clear, almost rhythmic now,
and he's conscious of the time of year—
the month, the day, his memory allows.
Soft needles cushion his footsteps.
He tries to whistle, to hum
and then to sing aloud
because he's lost and afraid
to be mistaken.
I am a human being,
he starts to chant
loud as fluorescent orange, he hopes,
I am a human being—
and he laughs between
each triumphant declaration—
not crazy yet,
just finding the words
he's needed to say for years.

THE PROFESSOR

let the pages ease from their bindings,
soar, buoyed by the miracle of language,
and stir the sky like autumn birds

BACK TO SCHOOL

August, month of the evening cricket,
the withering garden, the sun
tired of its expectations,
and you, the professor,
begin to dream of chalk dust
filling your lungs like coal dust,
or the dream of losing your classroom,
sprinting down corridors,
squinting at room numbers,
so far removed from the one you seek.

After a summer of casual drift,
you are suddenly aware, again, of your clothes,
your posture,
of what your face looks like
when stating a fact.
The sea of student faces
you are about to encounter
sends you searching for the Dramamine
you believe you have in the First Aid Kit
you took on vacation.

All you know, all your credentials,
begin to look like toenail clippings
someone forgot to throw away.
Characters from novels
you waited to read until summer
begin to usurp your subject matter—
your lectures threaten to turn into soap operas—
the heroine or hero making fun of your pedagogy
and landing in bed with your power point presentation.

What you do to help yourself
is buy school supplies
durable folders, pens with precision tips,
a planner that includes an alarm clock,

a new outfit for the first day of school,
a new skin, thick, flexible, familiar
as the wish you had one time long ago
to teach, to fill a room
with the beautiful sound of thinking.

PETITION FOR GOOD BOOKS

Let them be your noontime sandwich
nourishing, spicy, buttered with desire.

Let them line your walls and fill your arms
and tumble from your bedside table.

Let their magnetic power
draw the viewer from the frantic screen
and toward the shady maple.

Let the office visit and the traffic jam
be sweetened by their dialogue,
their stunning metaphor.

Let the margins be peppered
with WOWS and YESSES.
Let Highlighters set their best passages on fire.

Let them teach you good posture
as you balance them to bed
and then become your lullaby,
your final waking song.

Let their words become a lovely web
connecting you to early scribes
illuminating sacred texts
in gorgeous filigree.

Let their texture become familiar as skin—
a shedding, a new leaf.

And when the final book is ended,
let the pages ease from their bindings,
soar, buoyed by the miracle of language,
and stir the sky like autumn birds.

THE PROFESSOR KEEPS TRYING

Fingers twitch and text.
The classroom runs on electronic tension
while she unpacks a classic.
Now she's disturbed enough to scowl
and wish herself to 1983
when blackboards held authority.
With a sigh, she powers up her power point
colorful and bulleted,
vies for their attention in the darkened room
where she becomes the disembodied voice-over
and her class takes on the eerie glow
of screens up front and down below.

The professor says the names Becky and Ben,
Alex, Pete, Jay, Allison
with belief in their flesh and blood,
their real, real lives before them unfolding . . .
and she sees herself cutting invisible wires
startling the room from its virtual sleep,
hands opening up the *Norton Anthology*
to Blake's *Songs of Innocence* page one-thirty-three.

POETIC FORMS

Try a sonnet this time,
keeping true to your own voice—
no archaic diction, please.
The professor has spoken
and students begin their fourteen lines
as if the prompt were reasonable,
as if the sonnet, brief, prescribed,
unfolded like a bath towel
and absorbed emotion, cleverness,
music, a heartbeat.
Jason wonders if iambic pentameter
is required; Audrey thinks the form
is easy, finishes it off like a sandwich.

The professor looks over the drafts,
checking for sparks, a graceful turn.
Her hair needs cutting, her nails a clipping—
she could use a good night's sleep.
No time for the body, she laments,
as love and longing rise from the pages,
handwritten, as if meant for her.

IN PRASIE OF DISRUPTION

She has fallen into habits
durable as time:
paths she takes about the house,
food she eats at her familiar place,
the then and how of doing
what she daily must.
The cloth wipes clean the table,
a dish is put away,
the book opens with page folded
to mark the spot.

Ignition sounds—she drives to campus,
the route a vein on her right hand.
Students jostle in;
their sleepy eyes are half aware of her
and what they know.

Then, of course, disruption
wreaks havoc on her planned and
placid world,
hiding lists and lectures,
turning intentions inside-out,
revealing all their untied threads
and offering her a broken cup,
a useless vessel to do with what she can.

THE PROFESSOR IN THE COURTROOM

She's forced to manage her own face while taking copious notes. She can hardly stand to look at the plaintiff, whose demeanor gives her the creeps, and the defendant looks so wrung out she wants to ignore his sins and send him on a cruise. While the lawyers blather on and witnesses offer their brittle testimony, she prays for "beyond a reasonable doubt" and examines the tired old question: What is truth? Keats says *Beauty is truth, truth beauty, that is all/ye need to know on earth, and all ye need to know...* and thank you very much, famous poet who died when he was only twenty-six. She shudders and tries to imagine the whole spectacle as a musical—a thing of beauty—we the jury members hidden in the orchestra pit wielding our instruments, the judge with his silver baton, our conductor, the lawyers tap dancing with top hats and canes, the witnesses, a chorus, singing *The Oath* in close harmony, defendant and plaintiff in the wings, ready to burst onto the stage with fingers crossed for their rendition of *The Truth*—a duet so heartbreaking and beautiful, it would be all ye need to know on earth.

PROFESSOR'S HUSBAND DRINKS FIRE WATER
WHILE WATCHING THE GOLF CHANNEL

Professor's Husband Drinks Fire Water
While Watching the Golf Channel
could be the headline of her middle years—
something odd and metaphoric here.
Perhaps to sip his fire in the rough
will be a fire at least, will be enough.
Sonorous sounds of the announcer's voice, a pause,
a *thonk* of club on ball, polite applause
are what she hears from her judgmental perch
where she is doing her celestial research.
Though situated in his favorite chair,
he's on the fairway, he's on the air—
his swing precise and strong, he's lofted a Calloway
(St. Andrews green's a-shimmer on this sunny day).
It soars, then arches, drops—but not on Scotland's sod.
It's landed ever so gently in the lap of God.

PROFESSOR SITS ON STANDING COMMITTEE

The pulling in of chairs, the Chair seated visible to all,
water bottles, a few scarves, a tie, two sweaters,
the odd iPad, clearing of throats, a joke.
The minutes approved, the agenda referenced, a few sighs.
A motion, a second, a discussion, three yawns.
Sips of water, some looks across the table,
someone's cologne, a cough.
A self-important monologue regarding the faculty handbook,
the glazing of eyes, a cell phone bleats, a blush and snicker.
An earnest young face among the cynical seasoned,
a call for a subcommittee, a painful lifting of hands,
a reinvention of wheels, another proposal shot down.
The opening of planners, the setting of timelines,
some leave-taking behavior, the call of adjournment.
The pushing back of chairs, some niceties exchanged,
the thought of dinner lifting the shroud of what just happened.

HIGHER EDUCATION

The grades are figured now in neat and even rows.
Her students go their separate summer ways,
marching to their iPhones' magic tunes.

She snaps the dead wood from the old forsythia—
a breaking satisfaction, a clear decision made
in the muddle of final blossoms.

What has she taught these many years?
What works under this unanticipated sky?
Perseverant shoots, unfolding leaves,
insist their way into the broken world
against all odds, against all GPAs.

THE MESSAGE OF THE ANTS

*We are closer to the ants than to the butterflies. Very few
people can endure much leisure.*

—Gerald Brennan

The summer before she calls it quits
her retirement gleams before her like honey from the rock;
she imagines long days of reading, writing,
walking tours in pastoral countrysides.
Her deck chair positioned westward, shaded,
she examines her flip flops
and then she sees the ants.

So industrious they are—and so many,
scurrying about this treated wood
with ownership and purpose.
That one carries something she can't identify;
another simply explores, but what and why?
They carry on bravely
and seem to say *hello, goodbye* to one another
with those amazing pheromones,
polite, efficient little telephones.

Her snappy new flip flops want to squash them—
these creatures of nonleisure
invading her deck, admonishing her now to volunteer
at a homeless shelter, to take in refugees
and work and work to make the colony prosper.
For a minute, they bring to mind a poem by Whitman
and then she decides to forget the old bard
and get herself a proper glass of beer.

WHAT I CANNOT TEACH YOU

How to awake in the night
in harmony with darkness,
how to be grateful for
ragged days of winter,
how to love your life
even as its fire dies,
its ashes cool.

THE SELLER OF BIRDS

How do you know but ev'ry Bird that cuts
the airy way
is an immense world of delight, closed by
your senses five?

—William Blake
The Marriage of Heaven and Hell

I.

Here take this one
with the white feathers.
It will sing best in darkness.
You can sit on your porch swing,
hear the clear, sweet staccato
carry from the window.
The tangled trees
will enter the black
wash of sky
deeper with each note.
In daylight
the bird will tuck its head,
find the darkest place
within its breast.
By day a feathered heart,
by night a songbird
drawing you into darkness
deep enough to cover you
and the brightest stars.

II.

This crested one
will learn the circumference
of your familiar places.
Pay attention to its path,
arcing, then steady.
The unwavering rhythm of wings
will make you forget
the uneven traffic of your days.
The sky will bend
and you too will change
as if in the keeping of
an angel
who threatens to leave
or never leave you.

III.
This is the only
bird of prey I sell.
Look how these eyes
hold the gleam of the moon,
these talons curl
restless for the catch.
Notice the beak
made to pierce and shake
life from a creature
and lay it at your feet.
If the bird becomes yours,
the hunt will take you
like a fever.
At the snap of a twig
you will hold your breath,
your blood will rush
with the bird's descent.
In daylight the conquest—
a dance of fur and feathers,
but in the night the pounce and cry
will snare your dreams.
Fine pelts will comfort
your bed and house,
soft spoils of conquest,
reminders of your choice—
a bird that would kill for you.

IV.
Waterfowl, plentiful here,
are sold in pairs.
The birds mate for life.
In courtship the male preens
behind his open wing,
dazzling the female
with all the blues from coal
to winter sky.
He splashes silver arcs
as slowly she swims forward,
touches his bill,

the pact sealed.
Yearly the bond is tested.
Colors more brilliant appear
and with each attraction
you will fear their parting.
But always you will hear them
calling over the din,
breaking the water
in the same direction.
On the shore you will wonder
at your longing
as their wings slip through
the moonless night.

V.
And the shore birds.
One stands there
in the shallows.
Its double trembles
in the slow current.
The bird waits
for the shimmer of fish
through long afternoons.
If you choose to buy,
you will learn what waiting knows.
When your eyes meet
the fixed eyes of the bird
you will enter its sanctuary.
Here twigs pass like mourners
in the drift of a day.
Frogs and water bugs blink shadows
across the floating sky.
All things move without a push.
In this place
you can trace the curve
of neck and back,
the half-opened beak
against a sure horizon.

VI.
If you choose a scavenger,
you cannot be spared
its pursuit—
churning flesh
lifeless for days.
Nothing satisfies
like this feast
taken in the dark wind
of an open field.
You will shudder
as the bird eats its fill,
swings into the sky
to soar and dive itself
to emptiness.
You will follow
as it tracks the sick and lame,
your heart hardening in its wake
as you see your own swoon and fall
completing the spectacle.

VII.
Those with the lovely plumes
draw apart from the others.
The angle of the head
speaks of a vanity
deep within the species.
All day they strut and preen,
now and then
fanning the famous tail
set with emerald eyes.
You will own a showpiece
with this bird,
a creature hungering after
the admiration of strangers.
You will buy mirrors
to reflect the bird's exquisite display
and find your second self
there in the glass

with the bird
and the eyes that will not close.

VIII.
The bird in its nest
will soon be extinct.
For centuries
its feathers have been a prize,
its beak a medallion.
If you want the bird
you must take it to a secret place,
keep vigil on its nest,
its precious eggs
breaking to the last birth
of a kind.
You will tire
of the chirping young,
their throats clamoring
for the worm
like the most common species.
But as they grow
and drop from the nest,
the marvelous signs will appear—
iridescent wings,
the noble golden beak,
the tail that flames in flight.
You will trail them
through woods and fields,
count them over and over
as their shadows
cross your anxious face.

IX.
Here is a bird
that will mimic your voice.
Its close attention
to your speech
will silence you for days.
Slowly you will learn
to speak again,

listen for the bird's translation.
You will discover
what you are saying
for the first time.
The bird will ruffle
at your laughter,
turn its head
to your mutterings and sighs.
Your tone of voice
piped back at some odd hour
will set your jaw.
What the bird says
will matter more and more.
In time
you will speak a language
beyond imitation.

X.
The most faithful bird
is perched on the fence
near the willow.
It is ready for your message,
a prayer scrawled on a sleeve
or love letter weighted with sighs.
The wings will splay,
take up the rhythm
set by your heart.
It will brave wind and rain,
lightning that tears its path.
Above the raucous cities
the flight will slow—
bells and banjos sound from the square.
At last
in the stippled light of dawn
the bird will draw near its mark.
The message will be traded
with a promise or rebuff
and you will see the bird's return,
wings torn and straining
to reach your open hand.

WEST OF IRELAND

here in Ireland
this hand must learn to imitate the shore,
receiver of what will freely come and go

TAKING TO THE ROAD

Your feet will bring you
to where your heart is.
—Irish Proverb

Your young faces grow wise
in the newness of this land.
A journey through a foreign country,
the heaviness of packs,
and voices saying, *Come with me,*
I will show you the amazing place
your heart desires.
Your twenty years blossom
with stories and song,
landscapes and seascapes,
new friends whose words linger
like smoke.

From here you can go anywhere.
The winding stone-walled roads
have taught you a language
known to all on earth . . .
the confident stride,
the thumb pointing the way,
the memory shaping itself into words
that soon will fall from your tongue
like the rains of Ireland.

PADDY COYNE'S

Old women step dancing
at Paddy Coyne's pub
glow back into their youth.
Somewhere along the stem
of their lives
their men stopped watching
the twirling skirts,
the high kick in time
to tin whistle and drum,
and instead gaze deeply
into the frothy glass.
The women's hands join together,
their bodies weave
the remarkable space
they have created.
Their eyes shine into one another's
as they begin to spin,
hair flying, feet drumming,
the room a dazzle
of long—living women
embracing and holding on.

ISLAND WOMEN

Laugh of Sheela-na-gig,
wildness unleashed in the hummocks,
woman whose name is Ireland . . .
your sons die for the land,
your daughters remain invisible,
but the ancient mouths of island women
tell me who you really are.
Scathach on the Isle of Skye—
it was she who trained Cuchelainn
who sought her, learned from her
the skills that made him known.
She is the warrior difficult to reach,
whose island defies the faint hearted,
the acceptance of trouble.
She is the one who watches over the waters
saying *there*, and *there*, choosing those
deserving of her wisdom, dispensing her favor
in the flashing light.
She is the island woman I have come to know
despite the sorrowful adornments
she had been made to wear—
the shawl, the keen, the figure bent in prayer.
This woman laughs and sings
and ranges through these hills
she knows are hers.
Come look her in the eye.

COACH MASTER
for Owen

Through the eyes of tourists he thrills
at the formation of his own country—
its myriad of greens, puffs of sheep dotting the hills.
The woman in the red poncho exclaims,
Look at the rainbow! And they all do,
craning their necks, gazing dreamily upward,
asking him to stop for a photo shoot.

He navigates the narrow roads like a slalom skier,
gracefully dodging potholes,
fancying his coach a cradle
to gently lull his passengers to sleep
or sweet contentment.

Stone fences crisscross along his peripheral vision,
dividing up his dreams at night
between crisp sheets in some hotel.

Despite the weary hours, the endless stretch of pavement,
the sameness of the *oohs* and *ahhs,*
he will never tire of this land,
familiar and dear as his hand on the wheel.

SHEDDING

In another country
words overflow the brim,
you cannot drink them fast enough.
Smells of crumbling, burning earth,
velvet flavors, rich and dangerous
on the tongue, permeate each day.

Your quick hand hesitates,
forgetting its timing,
fumbling the easy pitch,
the handshake, the gesture.

You are a foreigner
trying to shed the too-warm coat
of your homeland,
trying to manage
in your own skin.

EMIGRATION

Here children run out the door to play
and never return.
They've watched their elders
stationed like dolmens
in the pub's blue haze
and felt the tether snap.
The Connemara landscape
gracing coffee table books
all over the world
has no hold on them,
their own restless pages turning, turning
after the disco strobe lights dim,
the dart games end,
after the last urgent push
of the school master.
England and America,
those well-heeled tourists,
promise to take them off the dole
and into the slick and glossy workplace.
Mothers and fathers
swallow the ancient keen
swelling in their throats
and turn back to the rhythm.

THE ELEMENTS

In the bogland, puddles and pools
each hold a version of sky
while hard sweating men cut turf
and drink and drink
the absorbing darkness of pubs.
Mists hover over the backs of sheep,
trail about the shoulders of mountains.
Waterfalls tinsel the country side
and feed the ocean
whose fullness swells
against jagged island shores.
All this drenching,
all this abundance of earth's sweet favor
in a place where thirst cannot be quenched.

BURREN

Under the parched face of the Burren,
rivers flow in caves and swallow holes.
Surface limestone, slabs in puzzle patterns
of a dry riverbed,
breathes the unseen living water.
In spring the botanist crouches
in this broken world
seeking the alpine flora: brilliant saxifrage,
delicate gentian taking a stubborn root
in any crevice holding a smidgen of soil.
She walks the lunar landscape
past portal dolmens—
signs of Neolithic farmers
who tilled this tableland,
her eyes trained on the dark, crooked spaces
where impossible life has found a way.

PORTENT

In the blue-black sheen of wings,
the watchfulness of eyes,
crows swoop the misty air,
perch on any horizontal,
always a band of them
menacing the landscape
with caws of darkness.
Here in the Connemara countryside,
your even pace slows—
a wariness, a hitch in the day
as crows gather too close
in the nearby field.
Their presence, names you *trespasser*
on this land of remote beauty
and slowly healing wounds.
Even when they lift into the sky
and disappear,
you imagine them punctuating
the winding road ahead.

COVERINGS

Watch him, watch him, that man
on a hill whose spirit
is a wet sack flapping about
the knees of time.
—Patrick Kavanagh
The Great Hunger

The skin of that distant hill
ripples over old potato beds
and covers the burning ache of men and boys
who cursed the clink of shovel on rock
and the wind blinding them to their task.
What was covered long ago
now and then heaves up into the light—
clean sprouts of memory tease bitter smiles
into old faces at the pub
and something close to pride
shivers through them,
coats drawn close, eyes hard as hunger.

TAKE

A photographer changes lenses
in the filtered light of a field;
her shoes sink into black mud,
her eyes squint against the lashing wind.
She has never seen
such texture in a landscape—
the punished surfaces of rock,
the soft luxurious grasses.
She forgets all she was taught
in art school
and snaps and snaps
these astonishing clichés.
A sprinkling of thin-legged sheep
pays no attention to the woman
or the view
but manicures the field,
sad black faces at work
keeping the land as it always was.

CELTIC DESIGNS

Lovers, drunkards, dancers
imitate the ancient patterns.
Dazzling tales
each strand of their telling
is woven by firelight
into the next.
Dierdre dashes herself
into the rocks for love.
Cuchulainn unknowingly slays his son,
the children of Lir are transformed to swans,
magic and treachery
winding them into their doom.

Atlantic waves emblazon themselves
on the surface of sand and rock
their crude and lovely leavings
ornament the shore:
filigree of shells and stones,
tangle of seaweed,
plastic shards, torn fish net.

Yarn held taut on the loom,
its strands mix and blend
as the shuttle slides.
Colors close in on each other,
melt in the scarf that will circle
a young woman's neck.
Her family name speaks of branches
wattled together,
of fortune bound to misfortune,
the weave tight but uneven,
fuchsia, gorse,
sweet flowers of briar and thorn.

Stacked stone walls
coil along country roads and over hills
weaving each traveler
into the Celtic design,
the rough course of history:
its patterns lost and found,
emerging as a scrambled maze
and again as perfect knot.

MWEELREA

A mountain named
to move the lips.
In the tangle of morning,
coffee steaming the window,
the heft of her glows through.
Sometimes a schmaltzy postcard,
backlit, hallelujahs bouncing
off her snowy ridges;
sometimes a hazy memory
fingering its way upward
into the conscious afternoon when
the newspaper read, sandwiches eaten,
Mweelrea speaks in a solemn pulpit voice
something of comfort and of warning.

Before a storm off the Atlantic,
Mweelrea smokes.
Dark wisps circle and glower,
hiding then revealing
her mountain bones.
Nearly transparent at dusk,
no longer grounded,
she seems to slip northward
in her gauzy shroud,
then vanishes.

In rare hours
Mweelrea projects onto the sky
in perfect focus,
her ridges now seams of an old coat.
Cloud shadows sweep
across her worn fabric,
clarify her textures,
gentle her curves.

For many days
I have watched her
shedding disguises like a fugitive.
Now, in the night
Mweelrea makes herself known
by blocking out the stars
on the horizon—

a formation suggesting a hand
sheltering the eyes,
a hand holding steady
in a baffling splash of Irish light.

SOUNDS OF INISHBOFIN

When the Island of the White Cow
rises out of the water
exposing its other self,
starfish sigh and stretch,
sea urchins fizz, crabs snip the air,
and overhead, a catastrophe
of gulls' wings and cries
awakens certain saints
long dead, who arrive in currachs,
their blackened bows
nudging island ribs.
But this is heard by no one—
only the driving tempo
of wood on goat skin drum,
the wild and urgent heartbeat of the land
is heard and felt in the night.

When the island stretches forth,
and subtle miracles occur along the shore,
all within range of human hearing
defer to the even pulse of laughter,
hard labor, and the heart's defense
played on the bodhran
by the middle-aged bachelor
waiting to inherit, drumming to live.

ON THE SHORE

On the shore
dusk-colored stones startle
with their perfect randomness.
Smooth, impassive faces
tempt the hand to touch and collect,
a hand that has disturbed this world too much,
rearranging the disorderly,
never leaving well enough alone.
Tidal pools exhibit new creatures every day—
sea anemone, razor fish, tiny crabs,
treasures to be shelved back home.
But here in Ireland
this hand must learn to imitate the shore,
receiver of what will freely come and go.

MWEELREA MOUNTAIN

This morning she stretches lazily across our vison,
wispy boa of cloud against white shoulders,
a tease, blushing slightly with Dawn's attention.

Restless by noon, she powders her face
and begins to pout, shadows ranging
across her sensuous curves.

Sulking now in the glowering cloud bank
of afternoon, she may emerge before sunset—
crowned, majestic in shimmering white—
or as a tent of darkness,
a cut-out against the Irish skyscape.

Dusk finds her steadfast,
a sister saying her goodnights all around
before Night takes her in his glittering arms
and carries her away.

LENTEN SEASON BEGINS IN IRELAND

Ash Wednesday, and the sky,
an unabashed frenzy of clouds and blackbirds
stirs up your mind, so intent
on quiet contemplation, on sacrifice.
The road to Lettergesh is dizzy with cars,
and you step off the road in time
to catch sight of an old man with a scythe,
arhythmically cutting the long
bristly grass of his field—
a staged picture postcard,
or a truth come home
on this day when labor doesn't cease,
or aging or need,
or the wandering mind
unable to hold still for death
to inscribe its mercy on your forehead.

AWAY

We hold our thoughts of home
up to the light like precious gems—
a friend touching death,
a father leaning in its direction.
They sparkle briefly in these
coastal towns, before we reach
the tourist office, the square
with its outdoor cafes, its forgetfulness.

Fourth vacation day,
our feet hurting on the cobbles,
our hearts singing in the warmth of Portugal.
We have arrived at the end of the world—
Cape St. Vincent, cliff bound.
Fortress and lighthouse, and eye to the sea—
haunt of Prince Henry the navigator.

More to the point, how to navigate
this dry land, this air
we're given, these aging bodies
drawn toward windless, rainless comfort.
Wherever we find ourselves—
close to shore or far inland—
our home is on our backs
needing repairs, the lawn overgrown.
This escape to a foreign sun in Lenten season
spares us for a time.
We have dressed in the gaudy costumes
of Carnival; its music's rhythmic current
carries us far from the dying body,
out to the other end of the world.

LIGHT OF THE DINGLE PENINSULA

His lips move
in the flickering light
of a dying fire—
prayers for the land, its people,
himself—perhaps mostly for himself,
cramped and shivering
through another spring storm.
Good Friday here must last forever.
This stone hut becomes
his crown of thorns,
his body pierced with cold,
his hands useless to illuminate
with quill and ink.
Below the cliffs, the ocean churns—
a jeering crowd calling his name.

VANTAGE

The peak of Croagh Patrick
appears as a smudge on the horizon.
The eye becomes a pilgrim
picking its way toward the summit
vaguely recalling the man,
the cross and the dizzying expanse
between this moment
and that agony.

A vein of gold
hides in the mountain's heart
and there are those who want it.
For forty days and nights
here St. Patrick fasted
and prayed in the bitter winds
of the Lenten season.

Clouds linger only long enough
to make us second guess our vision,
to mask the certainty of mountains.
Nothing the eye can see
from this cottage window
will be the same tomorrow.

PHOTOGRAPH

In a darkroom
far from Ireland
the Lettergesh road emerges.
Gorse bushes blaze
and twist toward the ocean.
Pebbles come clear,
inlaid like jewels.
But the camera eye
has favored the distance
where light collects and pools,
beckoning the human eye
to strain to see
what is about to happen
in the West of Ireland.

WORKING THE F-WORD IN THE WEST OF IRELAND

Would ya look at those f***ing daffodils!

—a local

Language proves inadequate to express
the delicious rawness of the West of Ireland.
It's so f***ing gorgeous:
mountains tumbling out of their beds of mist,
fields greening around the nibblings of sheep,
stone fences texturing the landscape—rickrack of dreams.
And how to describe the f***ers
who break into cottages, piss in public,
litter the countryside?
They are f***ing bastards, the lot of them!
If you are fall-down-f***ing drunk,
hope your mates will get you home to bed,
while your mouth runs its f***ing litany of f***ers.
Knock your head into a f***ing cabinet door?
The cabinet, the football—they are f***ers!
The face contorts, relaxes, shows its teeth
in forming that necessary fricative
that works to convey every last emotion
here in the f***ing West of Ireland.

VANE

The wind picks up,
levels a Kansas town,
dries laundry, scatters seeds,
enrages the Atlantic.
An Irishman chases his cap
to the edge of the sea.
The wind dies down.

SILENCE

What can I say
to this old man who
gives me a lift to Galway,
who scratches his ear
and sighs in a foreign tongue,
who seems to want me to talk?
The scenery is nothing to him,
a farmer, who wrestles the land
every day with a sorry heart.
I could ask about the weather,
when it will break,
what signs he knows of change,
or about the peculiar white rocks
lined up like sentries on that hill.
Would this sound contrived? Insincere?
What would I offer from my ordered American life
that would interest this man
whose worn hands
form a landscape all their own
against the blue steering wheel?
I can hear my voice make an effort
to remark or inquire
but it is too far away for him to hear.
My words fly back to the comforts
of their familiar places—
some white classroom or kitchen
where they fall effortlessly
on the ears of half-listeners.
And on this road to Galway,
I begin to learn silence
and its rare camaraderie.

NATURE

*it is enough to breath and touch
the solid bones of earth*

CONSIDERING FLIGHT

The readiness, the will
The heartbeat, the flutter
The stretch, the unfolding
The lift, the spreading
The weightlessness, the current
The wind, the light
The rain, the moon
The expanse, the unknown
The soar, the glide
The watchfulness, the ache
The circle, the mark
The imagining, the yearning.

LANDED

You are the bird still fluttering;
the exhausting skies ache in your wings
as if your freedom brings you down,
pinions quivering on a foreign perch.
All who envy your soaring and diving
imagine this moment as temporary
since so few know
the burden of flight.

APRIL

Today the robins
are fatter than ever.
Where are they finding food?
They waddle over the empty garden
pecking at nothing,
crazy old ladies
picking invisible lint
from their skirts.
April, and still snow flies
into the face of spring.
Fatness unaccountable
as a woman pregnant and starving.
She watches her arms disappear
while her belly grows large.
These robins are not well.
A closer look
and they are fighting
over what to do.
Fly back and wait?
Stay and die
in the bud-killing cold?
Huddle together,
form a nest of robins
to protect the orange bellies
about to burst with eggs?
The lies of April
bring a quickening,
then a stillness.
The crocus splits
and falls against the earth.
It is a time
to begin seedlings in the basement
to store woolens in chests,
to pretend.

CONTRAPUNTAL IN SPRING

Emerging from March
Sleeves full of tricks
Laughter and Stealth
Place salt in the sugar bowl
No scent of their passage
No help for the fools
Forever duped

The spies of April
Green with hunches
Rise from their winter bunkers
No qualms about intruding
On the innocent air
Forever hoodwinked
By this perennial trespassing.

THE GATHERING

A tree full of birds,
chirping branches bouncing
urgent mania of migration—
wings twitching stirring up November,
preparing the sky for departure,
exposing drifts of sunlight between clouds,
wind gusting east as winter circles overhead
like swifts around a tower.

SAID AND DONE

This is the last time I saw them . . .
bickering in the crab tree
in the new shine of morning,
tails whacking out their righteous
jib jab into my kitchen,
through my sleepy thoughts,
across my table, scurrying off
into the neighbors' maple
as if nothing happened at all.

TURNING

Birds carp at squirrels
in the mulberry tree.
Fruit falls into the grass
and is lost.
A ceiling fan
spins the lazy morning air
over the bed,
lifts small strands of hair
against the filtered light.

Last night the whir of blades
enticed a bat to enter.
It began its dark orbit
around the mechanical wings,
circled for hours
in a perfect concentric path
dipping slightly in its course
above the sleeping girl.
When once the sleeper turned and sighed,
the bat shied into a corner,
its webbed wings ticking the wall.
The room lost its attraction,
the sky threatened light.
The bat folded and disappeared.

Now the girl yawns,
opens her eyes to the mulberry tree,
the squirrels' chase, the birds' ruckus.
She stretches her thin white arms
and twirls and twirls,
her gown billowing
in the last rounds of childhood.

PUDDLE

Under the swing
after the rain
before you grow up
beyond this town
beneath your shoes
between your knees
between the chains
in rippling sky
in rippling mud
inside your head
with dreamy swoosh
with shimmering soles
with face in clouds
as mother calls
from far away
through sheets of wind
behind the door
'till you jump down
into the splash
into the world.

CHILDREN BY THE BIG LAKE

Alewives litter the wave-scalloped shore.
Counting the dead, counting the dead,
children step on them one by one,
their own skin scaley-wet with sand.

With tugs and heaves they uproot driftwood
and drag it, marring the canvas of beach.
They want to see the sand-hidden ribs
and touch the ruin of water and time.

At the sound of gulls their arms spread wide;
they rise and drop and soar and swing.
Their calls are throaty, coarse and wild—
the gulls take flight and wheel away.

Their eyes skip back, then back again
to the long blue thread joining water to sky.
THE END, they think, where waves grow thin
and colors sink when night comes on.

And from their beds they hear the waves,
their cottage is locked, their sheets are white.
They swim and dive throughout their sleep
then drift and tumble to the shore.

BEACHED

He moves
sniffing the salt air
angles off
into the shadow of rock
old man face with a shell
wave flips him over
into the light
belly of sunsets
leaf of sumac
kicking jewel
on white sand

DEER IN THE WORKS

At once
into hot traffic,
it caught my heart
like a fountain
up and over,
spiral hooves and all,
dancing on this windshield,
that,
eyes wide and white, I
craned
to see this spark from the forest
disappear from my rear-view mirror,
safe in the thicket
on the other side,
its tail a blinding flash
vanished last
leaving a star
floating on the highway
for miles ahead.

DISPLACED

Antlers ram my house,
batter the east siding,
then lock with the downspout.
Edging backward,
the animal
pries the metal pipe
toward the sidewalk.
All twenty feet gives way
and it clanks down Sylvan Street,
the monstrous antenna
throwing sparks
at children and dogs
who run howling to their homes.

We live miles from a forest
or zoo.
The dogs in this neighborhood
wear sweaters.
Nothing is wild in this place
long subdued by the leash
and the blade.

I gesture at the window
beckoning to the deer
now thrashing at windshields
and bicycles.
But what would I do
if he came to me,
this animal tangled in my house?
How could I calm a creature,
lost as I am
in some suburb far from home?

CUCUMBERS

This is the year of the cucumber
vines have covered my yard
where walking is a hardship
cucumbers big enough to trip on
rest under the foliage
ripening
bellies next to the earth
this community of cucumbers
I have raised for pickling
I should leave them there
let them live out their lives
reach the peak of their green
let their whiskers stiffen
grow too fat in old age
fade, fade
and soften.

Nobody eats a cucumber
in its natural state
it must be mixed
or creamed or pickled
it is a great indignity then
for a cucumber
to be taken
it has an importance
in its warm dark place.

But when I think
of the crisp white meat
the seeds that quench my thirst
like nothing else
on a day in August
I wonder
why I should be so tempted
to pick and gather
these firm green bodies
and change them
in a thousand ways.

LESSON ON BLUEBERRIES

Blueberries
are not blue
in muffins and pies—
more a plum,
African violet,
more a bruise,
the Badlands at dusk,
a tantrum.
Blueberries seep
through the fluted edge
of a pie
and no one talks
until it is gone.
Bears eat blueberries
in the woods.
In winter the bushes
leave stains in the snow.

RHUBARB

My father lopped off rhubarb leaves
in rhythm. I can hear the kunk
of the knife, the leaves drop to the ground.

I see him brandish a machete
in a jungle of rhubarb,
hack his way through the thick of it,
haul the biggest and reddest home
for simmering.

He tells of his journey
over steaming bowls of sauce—
how he was lost for days
in a maze of red and green,
nourished only by patches of sun
and the sour juice of his harvest.

From him I learn
the secret rhythm of the knife,
how to hack through fibers
in a single stroke,
bind the stalks so none will break.
He gives me his knife,
his sharpened blade.

DROPPING

Large as baseballs this year,
walnuts thump against the alley,
split and smear the walkway
with their acidic, blackened hearts.
Dog walkers take their chances
under this threatening canopy,
hardly expecting a concussion—
so ridiculous a possibility.

How to behave in such a world as this?
To step out boldly in the face of ruin—
to promise others there is nothing to fear?

Things do fall from the sky, drop without intent,
alerting us to what we need to say and do
before we, too, let go.

Call the neighbors, host a party,
require helmets and a dish to pass.
In this dropping season, and the rest to come,
at least be ready, if not able
to evade and rescue,
to learn the rhythms of disaster
as best you can.

DUTCH LANDSCAPE

On the road to Antwerp
the eye skims the landscape
proofreading for a random willow
or tired fence.
This earth is harnessed for good,
reclaimed from the sea
and wattled soundly.
Yet Van Gogh,
troubled with too much sight,
remembers breathing fields,
cypresses, clouds, and stars,
his still sad face
haunted with an unwieldy universe.
Mondrian made it plain.
As trees splay their first growth
across this apron of sky,
a blade sharpens on the whetstone.
Slowly the tree learns geometry.

JUNE

The neighbor's cat
stalks my garden.
Twining shoots of sweet peas
attract him most—
paws and whiskers
from another planet.
From this lawn chair
I can name many such attractions:
defunct television aerials
shifting in the wind,
the spigot of a lawn sprinkler
shooting in five directions,
new leaves of the dying elm,
rust filling their veins,
cottonwood seeds
travelling in schools
across my field of vision.
Someone needs to call the plays
of this June day,
and I'm trying it out
under the alien shadows
of my straw hat.

WAY OF THE SKUNK

Like rare flowers breaking through stone,
wild animals persist in this urban landscape,
remind us how survival, un-heroic and messy,
has the face of our ancestors—the stow-away,
the pick pocket, who managed to make way
for us to settle here, in this comfortable neighborhood
and forget who came first to mark the territory.

Their scent has permeated the summer,
invading our car, our house, our thoughts
like a cybervirus. The porch swing lost its welcome
in the twilight air.

The sense of smell is the last to go
as death plucks away
our knowledge of this world.
It draws us forward into the dark,
connects us at last
to a family we hadn't recognized
as our own.

PERENNIAL

No need to weed now
as green turns the color of smoke
and the ripe fall without fanfare.
Yet we tend to them, coaxing and sure,
unable to save them
in the lengthening dark,
but still aware there is a salvaging
under the guise of the after—
the newly ripe turning so fast,
we cannot keep up.

I have a bowl of the sweetest harvest
sitting here in my clean kitchen.
I guard it from fruit flies
dying soon after birth,
their persistence so avid
they drown in their own happiness.

WHEN FALL IS MISTAKEN FOR SPRING

When fall is mistaken for spring
the eye is tricked by evening light
and the fine delicacy of grasses
slow in their fading.
Trees of a certain species, birch especially,
maintain their shy and fragile
look of newness until the first snow
secures them into winter.
By streams and ponds
the rosiness of autumn's turning
may be taken for the blush of April.
But the body knows the signs of no mistaking,
those breathed and heard and felt against the skin—
the sharpness of October chill,
the temperature of stones,
the sounds of preparation—insect legs
and wings of geese—the battening down,
the rising up, the whisper of farewell
along the far horizon.

THE WAY IT IS

Winter is holding out this year.
Almanacs predict invasions
of storms or stars
yet nothing is certain
but new winter boots in the box,
the dog sweating in his coat.

Recall the sound
of metal on ice before the thaw,
grass green under glass,
the diggers discarding hats and gloves
heaving their weight into shovels
to chip away all that is not spring.
Nothing matters
but to muscle toward the green.

All the business
to bring on the seasons,
take them away
like courses in a meal.
When they're over
we wipe our mouths
and find a place to sleep.

SLEEP

There is a time before snow
when a weariness takes hold.
Lovers too tired to woo
sleep cold
in the comfortless stretch of night.

In the lull of passion
heart beats quicken
only with the drag of the rake.
The body drifts from place to place
looking for the storm windows.

When snow sticks for the first time,
whiteness stuns the lovers
from their sleep.
They fling the blankets
to the floor
and make the windows steam.

THE RIGHT TIME

Through white sidelong winds
I see your house
rocking
windows asleep
I know you are home
waiting out the storm
this is what I like
weather I can feel
down to the bones
weather that gets in my socks
lets me know I'm awake

You are not ready
for my intrusion
I come to your door
rap with the ice on my mitten
I hear you hesitate
you know
it is your crazy friend
the one
who won't let you alone
you know you must
open the door
and when you do
I sprinkle snow
in your hair
tramp it through your house
and bundle you up
each winter
I tell you
you can't feel warm
if you can't feel cold
and always you nod
and come

SNOW STIR

The snow
has finally stopped
I try to warm
the morning
with my coffee
listen for
the resurrection
I spoon more sugar
into the cup
and rings of liquid
lap the glass
the sugar melts
or settles

The warning
is vague
trees snap
then snow scurries free
like hunted rabbits
and wind
coffins everything
my house feels naked
the windows grow hysterical
and clocks
pick up
the rhythm
of the storm

I will never
grow accustomed
to snowstorms
there's something
of death in them
a cry of ancient Indians
too old to live
a song of swans
too delicate for the world
a cup
losing its liquid
in circles

TREK

Somewhere between the Isle of Skye
and your own back yard
land breathes water
in the jigsaw puzzle of dream.
The inhale and exhale
pieces itself into a hiking trek—
air so pure that muscles
feel no ache, the body feels no hunger.
It is enough to breathe and touch
the solid bones of earth
where drift and flow of rain and tide
fill furrow, crack, and gully,
limestone, brimstone, feldspar, gypsum—
each cupping its allotment.
Springs surface in unexpected gush,
sounding the vast exchange
where tread marks of hiking boots,
like perfect trilobites,
mark your passage
on this shifting landscape.

FOOTPRINTS

A blue moon,
the year of flowering bamboo
and year of the locust.
How the river bends,
birds migrate,
ants find sweetness,
how my heart longs for something more.
What to do
with what I do not know.

Watch me, Mom!
A crooked somersault,
a laughing applause.
Attention like this
we yearn for all our days,
our best efforts bringing such delight,
we're wrapped in loving arms
and held and held
for what we have to offer.

The city is miles back;
there is time to fritter away
making footprints,
time to trespass, to improvise.
Pick up a stick, chew on a blade of grass,
let the ironies be ironies.
Do not try
to figure out the earth
or what you will wear.

FLORIDA

Ocean winds make a stir
and fruit drops like hail
as ripeness blushes into the tropics.
Here in the salt air of Florida,
the sun droops, all its energy spent
swelling the mangos,
pumping citrus with enough juice.
In the swelter, orchids unfold.
Their scent staggers the ranging scorpions,
curls them into sleep.
Skins darken and grow thick,
the avocado, the retired mailman,
but nothing withers in this state.
Lizard eggs fly, fasten to endless bikinis
that rise at sunset to the flick
of tiny tongue and tail.
Gulls tuck in their heads
and bob with the Florida moon
in the waves all night.

WOOD SONG

Fine old wood
grain of Indian blood
I peel your bark
bore through your center
to find the ring
the season
I want to remember

Summer
welded days
nights blazed fireflies
everything was a secret
before I could see
in the darkness
you led me
on that crooked path
shhh in the willows
by the lake
we listened to the drums
your heart, my heart

From your wood
I made a canoe
I knelt in your hollow
you carried me
as far as you could
then we drifted

The water changed
from emerald
to diamond
your eyes a fire
a warning
I saw nothing
but ripples
behind your face

I felt you rock and crash
against my weight

from the lake floor
I could follow
the spinning of a moon shot down

I touch this ring
your wood
alive with insects
I listen for the drums
a loon breaks the silence
far away

THE REAL MUSIC

Here is the treble clef, troubled and without resources.
A melody enters from the left with something bright and promising.
Always, in spring this is the way—and yet, we forget
that grace notes, like the mind, have their limitations.
Forsythia and daffodils, their yellow stops and rests take over.
Nothing can deter them—not even Mrs. Dalloway.
Let's not put faith in those troubled treble notes
insinuating themselves into your piano or guitar.
The world is not solved, and we cannot make it so
unless there is some percussion, maybe a woodpecker
drumming its beak into the heart of the forest,
or overhead a flock of cedar waxwings drops and lands
on telephone wires forming a perfect chord.

THE MEDICINE

Coffee, saint of her morning,
draws her into the news, the shower,
and then the ache sets in,
nemesis to morning's promise.
It fumbles with her nerves
when she goes about her work.
The white oblong pills
cannot be swallowed soon enough
to give a short reprieve, and rituals
offer gifts from what she loves:
a pear and cheddar on a purple plate,
some quiet talk, familiar as breath,
hilarity passed her way from friendly regions.
She crushes self-pity like a paper cup,
but sometimes hears it crackle, trying to unfold.
From her window the leafless crab tree
freely shares her last red fruit
with jays and finches who hold them
in their beaks a moment before ingesting.
They seem to notice her
as she reflets on them—
birds who fly away with magic
in their wings.

PEARS

for Dana

Look how their ripening bodies
lean and shine
in the voluptuous October light.
The bowl cannot contain their curves—
they are threatening to expose everything.

When the painter mixes colors:
ochers, sunset reds, fertile greens,
the pears grow sincere and still,
winsome as homecoming queens,
ready to be fixed in the world
as they ought to be seen.

PORTRAITS

For all her time spent in mid air,
she might have attempted flight
or levitation.

ANGELA LIES IN A HAMMOCK IN THE SHADE OF A MIMOSA

Her hair is damp,
tendrils cling to her neck,
her right arm hangs in languid grace
over the side of the canvas boat.

Eyes closed, she softly hums
to music wafting from the porch,
a tune that glides into her
consciousness like the smile of the man
she soon will meet, sweet,
a little bashful.

She is in no hurry to make a move.
The summer day is all
that it was meant to be—
hot and humid, slow and lazy,
thick with possibility.

SCARVES
for Mary (1948—2015)

So many ways to tie, wrap, or drape a scarf—
an accessory that changes everything:
scenery becomes exotic or elegant—or maybe dizzying
if the pattern flies in the face of order.
There's Mary considering which one to wear—
her signature black clothing a canvas on which
flowers could bloom, suns could rise,
twilight could settle into night, or a storm could brew.
Wherever she has gone, she's left a trail of color—
scatterings of her brightness, her fire,
swirls of mischief, purple of bruise, blue of freezing.
There's a correct way to wear a scarf, she would say,
and demonstrate—her hands weaving the fabric
into complexity as she looks you in the eye
and smiles a love that swaddles and will not let you go.

EIGHT DEFINITIONS

There are certain ways
to fold the paper
when wrapping a gift
to make it uniform,
light, professional.
Women in department stores
do it with serious faces.
They are making mysteries.
They love their jobs.

Sleep that comes
after the dance
is a conversation.
The sleeper listens all night
trying to catch the words.

When women in Victorian novels
would say,
Let's take a walk in the garden,
it wasn't meant
they should tread
over rows of carrots and beans.

If you read a book
in the heat of summer,
the cover sticks in your hands.
Words arrange themselves
like jacks
on a sidewalk.
What you remember of it
is the smell of paper,
cicadas drowning out the birds.

Pans and glasses
stand in the sink
with water and residue.
Here is where the mother prays.
Some nights
she pours a brown rinse
through her hair
to cover the grey.
She is afraid
the children have seen her.

It isn't easy
to hoe between the rows
when weeds and rows
look the same.
It always sounds so easy
when people say,
Hoe between the rows.

Care has been taken
to open the gift
without tearing the paper.
In the box
is a silver cup
with your name engraved.
For a moment,
before you open the lid,
you are struck
by the silence of your guests.

If you find
one special thread
in a factory-made garment,
you can pull it
and unravel everything.

DENTAL ADVICE

Beware of the man
with perfect teeth.
That flash of smile
is a mirage,
a box of Chiclets
promising more
than it can give.
Look for the man
whose teeth
sidle up to one another.
His smile speaks of
intrigue, mutiny, revolution,
a puzzle with pieces
reluctant to fit.
He is the man
who chews his meat
with a vengeance,
whose kisses are sharp
and to the point.
In this world going soft
with keyboards and printouts,
it is good to find a man
with tempestuous teeth.

HE SHOOTS BASKETS FOR HIS LOST FATHER

The ball pounds out a message,
so it seems:
Another lay-up and he will come back.
From a room of books and filtered light
where plants outgrow their pots,
a neighbor tries to know
the baffled anger
scuffing through his afternoons.
Seen through a window
the boy becomes fragile
in the fiction of this room.
His shoes stir and grind
the broken pavement
into knots of dust,
his best growing years
drop through the net.

I AM SO TALL

I am so tall
I am first to see
men balding,
ripened apples,
leaves turning.
In winter
I make giant angels
in the snow.
I am so tall
I am headless
in bathroom mirrors,
doubled up in back seats,
singled out in group photographs.
I do not mind the distinction
the weather up here is fine.

A CROWN

Uneasy lies the head that will wear a crown.

If you will rule
you must see the valley below:
its breadth, its range,
its colors, its textures,
the mixture, the separations,
the sprouting and the dying,
the razed and the flourishing.

You must make a judgment about this
and hope you are right.
If you can sleep at night
in the whiteness of justice,
in the bed of deliverance,
you are unworthy
of the crown you have won.

TO KNOW THE HEART OF A TYRANT

To know the heart of a tyrant
you must study the eye of a housefly,
the mortar that binds brick to brick,
the path of the locust in fields of grain.
You must seek the shadows
and call them your neighbors,
your closest relatives.
The wind will be an offense
and the sun a tool.
What you ever knew of suffering
will become an award-winning film
acclaimed for its timing,
its beautiful camera work.

BIOGRAPHIES

You turn the pages,
enter each orchestrated chapter,
a neatly sorted famous life,
and begin to long
for your own table of contents
to have such order,
for a version of your life
to appear in print
and tell you
how one thing led to another.

The geraniums she loved
in her grandmother's window boxes
appear in her poems
as metaphors for fidelity.

In him she found the soul mate
she'd sought since childhood.

What a relief to see patterns
emerge from the jumble of your life . . .
the biographer kindly omitting
the banana peels, the backtracking,
huge expanses of wasted time,
offering footnotes,
an index, and a final resting place
in the Library of Congress.

OLD FILM

Two rolls of film
undeveloped found
in the back of a drawer
are placed on a crystal platter.
They float, buoyed by their reflections,
black cylinders holding the mystery
of faces now altered
or deep beneath the earth.
Some night the cat will stop his rounds
to consider these curious spools.
His leap will crack the crystal dish.
He will spin and chase
the memories all night,
the child's baptismal gown,
the grandfather's prize fish
whirling to the mischief of the hour.
In the morning
the crystal will sparkle
like never before,
new facets throwing broken light
across an angry face.
No sign of the old film
tightly coiled
in the back of a mind.

FEET

This woman I see every day
keeps looking at my feet.
I always thought of them
as ordinary—
attached to the end of my legs,
five toes each,
tucked into long wool socks,
slid into shoes.
Until now
I was never aware of my feet.
They took me where I was heading
without complaint,
adapted well to the weather
bare or booted.
Now they become interesting,
a main attraction.
I watch them
at the end of my bed:
two old ladies
nodding a silent conversation,
two newborn kittens,
eyes closed,
two forty-year-old feet—
veins like blue lightening—
follow them to my heart.
Extraordinary feet.

FACING UP

After your chenille bedspread
went threadbare
and you'd liked Ike
as long as you could,
you lost your
peripheral vision
behind long hair

Your black arm band
stalked to and from
the capitol
finally landing
in your socks drawer.

It's time to see yourself
as you are—
blonde furniture of the '50s
leaning a bit to the right
without knowing it.
Watch yourself
in old cartoons,
Daffy Duck
lost in the marshes
wandering witless
through cattails
as guns blast the sky apart.
Your only hope now
is to find your way
off the screen,
get a better job,
forget about it.

SURE THINGS

I schedule
to meet a photographer
who wants to catch
my breath on film
on the way
I straighten my hair
in a store window
someone watches me
from the inside
when I notice
my eyes wander
from the reflection
I look into the eyes
of a stranger
until they can look
no more
later I bare my arm to give blood
I am so still
yet this pumping
listen to the intervals
steady as the crickets
rubbing their bones
into the night

FALLING

If I were the moon, I know where I would fall down.

—D. H. Lawrence
<u>The Rainbow</u>

She kept records of her falling:
age five from climbing bars
slippery with rain,
at twelve from an excursion boat
on the Fourth of July.
She fell from a rearing horse
at sixteen.
Newly married,
she fell down basement stairs
carrying tomatoes and clothes pins
and later from the back porch
reaching a firefly for her son.
On and on she fell.

For all her time spent in midair,
she might have attempted flight
or levitation.
Instead, she dropped through space
without glory or intent,
simply fell, gathered herself up,
and carried on.

SOMETHING ELSE

What is it
keeps tugging at my sleeve
I'm old enough and married
could have three kids by now
cut my finger on a can
thought about it for three days
what is this
I'm feeling well
put myself together
go to work
but what
comes blinking in my head
at night
and now more often
as I go about my business
something tells me
it's time
for a change in weather
and that's okay with me
the second coming was scheduled
for 1948
the year I was born
no one I know
was disappointed
but it's going to happen to me
I feel it now and again
as I water my plants
pull on my boots
something gives way
a china cup
falls from the table
a clump of snow
melts on the hardwood floor
these are good signs
to one who was starting
to settle in

FINALE

The conductor's baton suspends,
sustaining the final note.
Faces perspire among the chorus,
instruments gleam,
all sound sweeping toward the shore.
In the patch of silence to follow,
the pianist rests his eyes on the score,
hands afloat above the keys
before the storm of applause.

CONFESSION

A March holiday in Florence—
all those Guccis
easily clicking on cobbles,
Italian men slowing at window displays
to note their reflections among the glitter.
My camera eye will not take in the expanse
of the cathedral, its marble glinting delicious colors,
its dome umbrellaing us all.
Then, turn the corner, and there they are—
three sweet faced women from somewhere familiar
in peacoats, bright scarves, and sneakers
confidently singing American show tunes
in the closest harmony,
their basket filling with Euros,
their snappy music washing down the antique streets.
I confess these displaced Madonnas from home
touched my compromising heart
more than all the riches of the Renaissance.

IMAGINING ROME

All roads leading there,
and me still lost,
the Vatican's cold shadow,
the Forum's rubble,
the Pantheon smelling of sweat,
neck and shoulders aching
from looking ever upward.
Soon I will be walking those cobbled streets,
money disappearing like dew in sunlight,
emperors glowering from pedestals,
tour guides valiantly drawing our attention
to another Madonna and child,
another tired story to bring antiquity to life.
My feet are blistered, I've lost my glasses,
wine-dehydrated, leery of pickpockets—
Parla Inglese? I need to go home
even before I've arrived.

BODY

Your body is a suitcase on rollers
containing all that matters.
It negotiates the roughest terrain
but someone, God bless him,
has organized the contents in plastic bags.
Systems churn and pump in there—
pipes and veins, arteries,
serving up and circulating.
Then there are the nerves—
each tiny, sensitive tributary
potent enough to send you over the edge.

Yes, I saw The Body Exhibit,
the controversial display travelling the world.
The place was packed but quiet as a library.
We moved from body to body,
from displays of particulars—healthy and damaged,
to cross sections—bones sawn with clean precision.
Amazed and alert to our breathing, roiling selves,
we walked into sunlight, pavement more solid
to our precious soles—each joint and tendon
performing like an orchestra.

So I try to find an analogy—and a suitcase it is—
unscientific, urbane, necessary.
Someone is pulling this suitcase along—
over bridges, through tunnels,
across deserts and busy highways.
It tears and rumbles, the zipper breaks,
contents spill, are re-contained.
This miracle, this body, rolls along
at times oblivious, but right now,
in the ink of this moment, its heart is moved,
its brain sparks gratitude.

HAIR

It's what we pat or shake or swipe away
when guests arrive,
this hair we're given
to part and cut and color, braid and spray,
its claim on us so strong we'd crawl
through snow and ice to have it cared for
by the only soul besides our mothers
who gently washes, tends it while
we tell this mere acquaintance things
we'd never share with even closest friends:
what he said and how she left,
what you think about your tiny ears,
and how you're going to be more brave.
Somewhere hungry women
are braiding one another's hair—
strand by strand, they concentrate
on the pattern, the feel of it between their fingers,
these numbered, necessary hairs.

THE CELLOS OF OCTOBER

The cellos of October
accompany this blue and golden day
and those that seem aggrieved,
dissonant in restless winds, unresolved.
They elicit sighs and longings from the trees,
and sweatered walkers sway
to the deep, lovely forebodings.
Soon enough the oboes, then bassoons
enter in frigid air of minor key,
stirred by currents and kettling hawks.
A garbage truck rumbles down the street,
brakes, lifts and dumps;
bins drop, the snare drum snarls
along the curbs. Bodies hunker down
as the French horn sounds a plaintive phrase,
sweeping the landscape into
its final pianissimo.

WHILE FIGURING OUT TOMORROW

for Pamela

While figuring out tomorrow
her list lengthening,
her stomach, a relentless knot,
the day shrugs and moves on,
its lazy clouds drifting and mingling
over her anxious head.
Three neighbor girls
swing past, their giggles
rattling the windows of her intent,
and she writes *change water*
in hummingbird feeder.
If she can control the weather,
the birds, others' regard for her,
she can rest in the hours she is granted,
but she knows there is no harnessing
the clouds or a net large enough
to hold the birds close to home.
She is left with the bright red zinnias
on her kitchen table overseeing her list,
whispering comfort
from the hands that bestowed them.

UNCERTAINTIES

The weather here
is tricky
one day warm and brittle
another sloshing you about.
This weather
I can't count on
gives me no rest.
My umbrella
has quit understanding,
refuses to open.
Now and then
I lie awake at night
listening for signs
even check the sky
at intervals
for change of scenery.
But somehow
I never catch
the invasions of storms or stars.
I fall asleep
troubled
not knowing what to expect.

Today I wear a scarf.
It is warm
about my neck and shoulders.
The wind
has changed since morning,
blows from the north,
slams my screen door open
when I am away.
As I walk,
I watch the confused leaves fly,
catch in the gutters
or lie in fragments on the pavement.
Leaves cling to my shoes and
I carry them into my house
hoping to save them.

HOUSE

The tenants switch on lights
long before dark.
Their small rooms
lean together
and the eavesdropping begins.
In number one
the tap turns on and off.
In three the fry pan spurts.
The bed creaks in six.
The manager smokes in two
wishing away the tenants
and their noise.
>He sees the house whole;
>its bannisters
>guiding the family
>down for their meals,
>up for their beds.
>Shades of carpets and draperies
>deepen with the hours
>and fires are lit.
>In the library
>he passes his finger over volumes
>in the flickering light,
>rings the maid for his brandy.
Smoke curls through the room
with no place to go.
He breaks a small pane
to let in air.

KING OF THE MOUNTAIN

Snow seeps up our sleeves,
down our boots,
stings wrists and ankles
into action.

The king, mittens caked in ice,
face a crinkled cabbage,
menaces with imperious shouts,
his galoshes flailing
like desperate fish
as he ousts us one by one
from his summit.

He has only to skip a beat,
slip on the hardened skin of snow,
and a new power will emerge,
sure as a red scarf
abandoned on the hedge—
bold rage of winter,
bright flag of spring.

ICE FISHING

In each shack
a man drops a line
through a hole in the ice.
Sometimes he opens his thermos
but mostly waits,
tempting the casserole of walleyes.

A story passed among the fishermen
says a dog slipped through a hole,
nosed its way to the opening
in a neighboring shack.
The dog, half-frozen,
split the drowsy silence,
its black head filling the space,
ears lifting like gills.

Dazed, the fisherman probed
at the creature
and knew it was a dog
when fangs lit the dark rectangle
and widened into shivering fur.
The man wrapped the dog in a blanket
and headed for town.

Behind his pick-up, the waiting goes on.
A bobber jerks,
a fish fights the air,
a man removes the hook,
drops back the line all in a motion.
All winter he dredges the water,
caring little for the catch,
lost in a whirlpool of hunches and dreams—
fish dogs, mermaids, leviathans.

WOMAN ON A SLED

This is her last ride,
the one flat on her belly,
face first into stinging whiteness.
She is arcing
over the rise before the river
where all sleds stop short of the broken ice.
After the flat stretch she hears
the runners she waxed so well
crashing over the frozen waves
and cheering
somewhere up on the hill.
She knows the river
never freezes over
but she will not drag her feet.

COMMUNITY AND FRIENDS

new filaments joining your own,
becoming you

BECOMING

In the folds of each day
someone waits to enter your life,
to appear in person or in a dream
and change you slightly—
as if a pencil sketch were being drawn
of you, and a line extended or erased
increases your vitality, your presence in the world.
Be ready for the entrance of a stranger
or a friend who, after an exchange, lingers
in the form of words, a look, a gesture,
new filaments joining your own,
becoming you.

WINTER WORLD
for Lucie

Falling snow and glimmering stars
confuse the eye on this midwinter night.
It looks as though a mother and her little girl
enjoy a walk with their unleashed dog.
Or is the child skating,
her red coat with fur-lined hood
confining her to tiny glides,
her mother helping her to balance?
An older brother pulls his sister in a sleigh
past a stand of giant firs dappled
with clumps of white,
though it could be groceries
being hauled along,
the boy a grandson helping out.
And then a trio, school friends,
laughing, holding hands,
tread the snowy path,
their scarves, bright banners,
flying in formation.
Or perhaps the center one is the mother
who suggested they go caroling.
Their timid voices grow stronger
as their boots pick up the tempo.

This lovely fiction, a gift from the artist,
is painted on the surface of a bauble
with the tiniest brush.
My eyes squint
to enter the happy scenes,
the tassels on my bright green hat
aflutter as I skate round and round,
breathing in the air
of this perfect winter world.

COMMUNION

Apples, bananas,
there is joy in your gathering on my table.
This apple
leaning into the curve of a banana,
this banana
joined with his brothers,
celebrate the morning
delighted with themselves.

COFFEE SHOP

Everyone's swiping at screens
as if to clear away dirt or fog,
as if this, no, this, no, this
will ever be the body's theme.

Outside it snows—the slow drifty kind,
while plows gas up, ready for clearing,
scraping clean for all to carry on
as usual.

Cataract surgery five springs ago
left me astonished at the sharp edges
of things: words, pages, leaves, the cross hatching
on my chin and brow.

A cup in my right hand,
its lip smudged by mine,
holds the reason I am here—
or is it instead, the company of those
who keep diligently searching
for a perfect window, a clear view.

HOUSE GUEST

I like to think
the one in the guest room
has a leather bag
lined with brushes
for every purpose,
shoe trees,
the most complete vanity case
bearing fragrant oils,
powders and creams.
I like to lie in our bed,
listen to the turning
and beathing,
imagine him
sinking deeply
into the comfort of this house
sleeping more soundly
than ever before.
In the morning
we will breakfast in the kitchen,
the rolls will be warm,
I will watch him
from the corner
of my eye.

KEEPING UP

Someone always runs ahead
turning now and then to check your distance,
measuring the gap between you.

Even the elderly compete, who once ran the block
for the fun of it, through Mrs. Vance's back yard,
around the old fuel tank, into the waving laundry,
shirt sleeves swiping their shoulders.
Now they're standing up for the hymn
on their first try, keeping an eye on their peers
in the pews ahead.

Plenty of time to keep track
of where you are in the line-up,
but so tired you are.

Whatever the reserves, an ache remains
to become Queen of the Mountain,
stationed at the top of the heap,
to have bested your friends in the garden,
planting and weeding as if spring were not enough.

LOSING YOU, MY LONGTIME FRIEND

for Rosemary

Your illness touches
all my favorite spaces—
my morning walk
is slackened by your ache.

My kitchen window weeps
and sorrow bakes a pie.
This book I read is empty,
the music's out of key.

I feel your quiet passing,
your leaving wrings me dry.
How can I see my own life through
without the grace of you?

MARY JANE

She told me once how
she and her younger sister,
on their long walk home from school,
made a habit of lifting
discarded Christmas trees,
dragging them home,
tinsel shimmering, sap
staining their mittens, needle-
strewn wakes wavering behind them.

They marveled at the many shapes
of evergreens, their back yard
stocked with them, stacked
to build a fort or laid out
to fashion freight trains or rooms,
their prickly boundaries hiding their private glee.

This was the early '50s when children
were left to themselves.
She said what makes the memory so clear
is the piney smell, infusing itself
into all the rest of her days.

Mary Jane, her life now closing,
gave me this gift—
the story of salvaged evergreens,
a parable of her long and fierce desire
to keep Christmas alive
against all odds.

RETURNING

On the tin whistle
he plays what he recalls of Ireland.
The tune darts
through the Michigan neighborhood
in the melt of March,
slipping now and then
on a patch of ice in shadow,
gracing the early spring air
with a reel and a jig,
medley of mountain streams,
of sunsets, bursting storm clouds,
of the steady ocean wave curling
back toward the familiar theme,
of pebbles, shells, and gulls glistening
against Glassilaun strand.
His fingers leap, his strong breath sustains
the spiraling memory
even as his heart begins to empty
into the sweet, sad, melodious clichés
that make old emigrants weep,
new emigrants mock and parody.
The neighbors open their doors and listen,
drawn out of their fitful winter thoughts
into the greening Irish song.

SHE WONDERS ABOUT THE NEIGHBORS

She wonders about the neighbors—
their sweet dispositions and hopefulness,
small children tipping over in bright snow suits
as Papa carefully forms an igloo.
The children cheer
when the snowplow passes by,
clearing a path just for them.

Coffee is brewing, her orchids look healthy,
and snow glitters around the children
cocooned in downy coats and snow,
so safe she cannot imagine them exposed
to a cold world of machines
grinding and whirling, no one steering.

NEIGHBORHOOD

Today the sidewalk blesses me,
leading my sneakers through corridors
of houses, trees, and flower borders.
The sky is teeming with a sea
of clouds and urban birds flit overhead,
crisscross the street and land on wires.
I hear young children laugh, the screech of tires,
a radio forecasting weather, my own methodic tread.
I feel the fortune of connection
to all I see and smell and hear
this green and golden day, this time of year
when loss seems small and grief an intersection
where I can cross or not, depending on the route
I take back home, how far I venture out.

SUCH A PORCH

Such a porch
to hold a happy crowd
in the magical time before cold
drives us in and darkness paints
us lonely and restless.
Such a porch for watching
neighbors in their everyday,
minding dogs and children
who think they want nothing more
than to be released
into a field or playground
with no one beckoning or warning.
From here the leaves unfurl and then cast shadows,
turn, and drop while we remark
about our beautiful porch,
its many visitations, the way it harbors
laughter and tears under its eaves
even as illness camps on our doorstep,
an uninvited guest refusing to leave
such a porch as ours alone.

PARENTS AND BROTHERS

the sweet ache of this world, . . .
the mom, the dad, the kids,
become more precious by the minute

THE DAWNING

I can't understand the words,
is what my father complains
on the first day of the new millennium.
We are on the phone, and he refers
to his grandsons who play music
and call themselves Future Primitive.
What ever happened to the message,
he wants to know, the content, the idea.
Some of us stored up food and water
to brace ourselves against a break-down,
some even purchased generators,
so ready we were to continue
just as we had been—
and so far everything's the same.
I process this poem without a glitch,
the cursor leading me
into language I can change
with a prompt from my brain,
a slight tapping on keys.
The message, the idea, this is
where I'm stuck.
Impressions of the world,
a gesture in the dark,
a flutter of truth,
maybe a kind of future primitive,
Dad, telling us there's nothing new to say
in words, and so we murmur our desire
in code as simple or complex
as your daughter's love for you.

CHOOSING A MONUMENT

He lays out the granite samples
like a game of Solitaire.
Agates wink out of the polished surfaces.
My father clears his throat
and moves his chair
closer to the display.

Agates—I think of them gleaming
in the shallows of Grindstone Lake.
We kids waded
watchful as herons,
scanning the mosaics around our feet
for agates, squinting
in the Minnesota summer sun.

Didn't we run to Mom then?
She was on the blanket in her pedal pushers,
her hair a wonderful mess in the wind.
Look at how many I found!

But when our small hands opened,
the stones had dulled and muted.
Nothing to look at, really.
But Mom would look and look and look again
our hands opening before her,
years into the future—
with something or nothing to show for ourselves.

And now, as I help my father
choose a fitting stone
to mark her place,
I want to gather up these granite wafers
and skip them one by one
across the lake of time
and show my mother
how stones can conjure up
her watchful eyes, her constant love.

FAMILY REUNION

That was the time you fell
between the dock and the boat
and had to be fished out
in front of all the campers,
he remembered
and I felt the embarrassment
all over again, laughing and comparing
the jaw lines of my brothers,
now in their seventies,
mellowed and a bit paunchy.
It's June, and cottonwood seeds
drift past the in-laws' yawns
on and on into the late afternoon
when stories singed with homesickness
spread out like fans
in this time out of time.
Embellishments and downright
fabrications dangle in the waning light,
wine glasses nearly empty, and
wasn't that the third time mom washed
out your mouth with soap that day?
And now I am wishing we would hear
her calling us in from the dark,
her soft southern accent tracing
our names through the neighborhood,
us sweaty from play in that time
that passed us by before we knew it.

227

MOTHER

I see you standing in the wind
by the clothesline,
a clothes pin in your mouth.
You are concentrating
on the white sheet
billowing before you.
Your thick, dark hair
is flying away from your face—
and suddenly I see you
as a school girl.

The clothes pin is a pencil
and you are thinking hard
about musical notes on the clef,
listening
as your marks on paper
shift into sound,
your faith nudging each chord
toward a perfect resolve.

The clothesline is now full
of the white gleam of the sun,
and I am blinded by this memory
and the fluttering of things
I have known about you
and almost forgotten.

MY FATHER'S MEMOIR

It is finished, spiral bound,
pages heavy with gratitude, judgement, confession, and love,
fact and fiction playing hide and seek
between text and photographs—
this one of Grandfather August, in his instrument shop—
Swedish, cocky, and surprised, circa 1904.
Unfinished violins, mandolins, ukuleles
hang in rows like elegant possums.

I find myself within the pages,
an infant held so lovingly,
my mother's face immersed in mine.
I grow up in the sweep of ministerial prose . . .
my father's children, collectively, make him proud.
The building years are neatly stacked
milestones as he sees them—
nothing teetering or fallen.

Stationed now in the small room
for which he pays dearly,
and cared for by strangers,
my father often dozes,
uncertain where time has gone.
He fumbles with the call button,
remembering that help is sometimes
at his fingertips.

Even so, the memoir still unfolds.
He's won a spelling bee with *sanctuary*
the deciding word.
At ninety-three he's taken up his old harmonica,
and plays again the tunes that manifest his moods,
his undaunted inner life.
He's gone to visit Margaret,
the one with no one left.
In her dark and stuffy room,
his glasses reflect her puzzled face,
and he remembers he has more to tell.

PART OF IT

for my mother

A dozen plastic zoo animals.
She wants to throw them away
but picks them up,
drops them in a box,
closes the lid.
Clutter under foot, on the calendar,
in the night
when even her dreams
stumble on one another.

She finds her make-up
gouged and smeared along the tub.
She knows the children are hiding.
In the mirror she watches herself
prepare a face for war.

She hears the wind-up toy
rattle under the sofa
with its last tinker-tink.
The sound stays with her
through piano lessons,
through dinner.

From the window
she sees her children
hitting trees with sticks
as leaves twirl against a mottled sky.
They think they make the leaves let go.
In a way, they do.

PETITION

Mother
we are sorry
we have taken from you
the workings of your clock
each of us
carries a jewel
with guilt
we stumble home for visits
each of us in turn
attempts to be heard
but always
when we speak to you
our words translate into cries
of newborn babies
you are happy
to give us milk
and none of us
has courage to refuse
time and again
we call to you
listen mother
this is not who you think
our hair is turning grey
like yours
we have seen everything
you hid from our eyes
we are old
older than you
perhaps know
with what you will not see
you draw us back to yourself
in steady pilgrimages
to make ourselves known

This is not the girl
who cleaned and cooked
by your side
watched you flute the edges
of a pie with envy
stayed home on weekends

and cried because she was so tall
look at me mother
I want you to see
what I have done with your jewel
I have made it worth more
than you imagined
I have grown away from myself
as you knew me
happy
in the body you gave me
in the long limbs
I once found impossible
see I stand straight
and I know so many secrets
I would like to tell you
will you never let me

SICKNESS

Mother I ache
I am swollen
pick the walnuts
ever so carefully
I hear you
my veins close to the skin
like yours
one kettle whistles
like all the rest
I hear it in my sleep
and animals
the cat in the hall
complains in five-second intervals
the dog next door
in three
mother
rub it here and here
make it better.

AS A SCHOOL GIRL

As a school girl
her mother's biting words
withered her, and she tasted
the bitter bile of her own hatred.
She knew she could not forget,
would never forgive or shrug them off
like her back pack, heavy with books.

How strange now, when years
have pressed their bitter patterns
into her mother's face,
to find herself on her knees
clipping her mother's toenails,
years of rancorous words
falling to the floor one by one
between them—
oddly beautiful crescent moons.

SHUT UP

Oh, the taste of a soapy tongue
returns, the wrath of my mother,
her face crumpled with her child's
barbed offense against another
human being, a precious soul,
a child of God. She, no stranger to
punishment, fought the good fight
of raising us, the divine offspring
of the church, our father a
minister of the Word, a copy
of the Testaments safe
in his keeping.

The neighbor kids, uncontrolled,
swore a blue streak across our yard,
no voice to stop them flying
to the creek and beyond,
when only hunger drove them home.

Our home, in this remembering time,
becomes a house, shut up,
the word with new consequences,
its aftertaste lingering on our
restless, fearful tongues.

YOU SHOULD PLAY THE VIOLIN

Shame on you,
my mother would say.
You have to practice
your violin.
And back to the music stand
we marched,
drawing the bow
to make the scale shrill,
a mosquito closing in
on the ear at night.

And so we became a family
of violinists
sawing our way toward the bone.
When one of us struck home,
the others picked up the tempo.
When the music said *rest,*
none of us did.
Soon notes flew off the clef
like birds from wires
startled by a change of weather.

Now I try to shame my son
into embracing that fine wood.
If he complies,
I will join him,
taking the harmony,
second violin.
If he refuses,
I will go to the symphony,
watch my mother
wield her magnificent bow,
strike the strings,
make them mind her.

CHILD OF THE QUEEN

for my mother and my son

My mother's back to me as she directs the choir—
her thin arms lift the voices higher and higher.
At this moment she is the queen and I am not her child.

Who is the child of the queen? I wish it were my son
whose heart is a broken vase he fashioned lovingly,
whose mother has no power to make treaties or make war.

No power to declare, but perhaps to shake the tree
and see what fruit will fall—to shake and shake—
the blemished and unblemished tumbling at her feet.

And blemished are the days I doubted Mother's love
her back to me directing all the voices except mine.
She let my song run wild, to be the voice of lost and found.

A song run wild, a son, betrayed, who films his tears
and makes them public works of art—
gorgeous, cinematic flows of sorrow.

The queen has finally raised her scepter
and I speak—her daughter once again.
I now will make petition for my precious son.

THE PREACHER'S KIDS

Summers we ran free, out to the woods
to the creek, and waded to the culvert—
dark passage to where? We'd only gone halfway.

On hands and knees we tried again, spelunkers
tunneling under the railroad tracks,
laughter echoing like the trumpets of the Lord.

Though expected to be exemplary we headed underground
dreading electrocution by the hand of God,
yet—we hoped for the spectacle—horror movie of the disobedient,

each of us set on finding the light
though we might be washed away,
though the journey was slow and painful

at a time in our lives when we had no idea.

WE ARE MISSIONARIES TO AFRICA

My parents have chosen to die
deep in the dust bowl of Kansas,
where dust to dust is no figure of speech.

My father's sermons,
still coming to him at eighty-three,
are filled with personal anecdotes.
He sprinkles them into scripture
like holy sugar.

Recently my brother found a photograph
of the two of us
dated 1949.
He is five and I am two, dressed oddly
in frumpy hats and too big clothes.
On the back my mother wrote:
We are missionaries to Africa,
words my older brother declared
after dressing us for the journey.

Immortal souls are fine
but the sweet ache of this world,
this skin, these dress-up clothes,
the mom, the dad, the kids,
become more precious by the minute.
Where our bodies will go from here,
to dust or to the Congo armed with bibles
and cast-off clothing, or somewhere else
is bothering me just now
as my father in Kansas removes his glasses
and thinks hard
about the new heaven and the new earth.

BUTTER

I can see it
a plate of soft butter
gashes full of jam and crumbs
mom kept it in the cupboard
to keep it soft
how we jabbed at that old ruin
plastered up holes
in Aunt Ida's warm bread
made wells of it
in our oatmeal
we always knew
where to find that butter
we loved it
weren't ashamed to spread it thick
on pancakes
anything we felt like
that butter was so good

QUARTET

Sing it through again lads,
loosen those bow ties
and shake the rafters
with what happens man to man
when nothing matters more
than carrying your part,
keeping in sync,
listening to your fellows
with a sympathy
beyond the range of song.
In this fraternal spectacle,
ego and ownership
are overruled
and the rare negotiations
of four part harmony
offer justice for all.

BROTHER

The one without guile
owns the tallest ladder.
Escape or Rescue
make demands like spoiled children.
This brother climbs into harm
higher, higher,
with the angels.

PROSPECT

Here is the desk
I advertised for sale.
It needs a coat of paint,
two drawer handles,
and a lot to fill it.
They keep calling
about the desk.
Is it oak?
How many drawers?
Why did you paint it?
I don't understand the questions.
I am over thirty,
my friends are all divorced,
my bills are scattered
on the basement floor.
This is the time for selling,
everyone says.
Get rid of your junk,
your husband, your old religion.
Get yourself a new desk,
roll top, walnut,
with lots of compartments and drawers.

I can barely hear the telephone,
so much noise.
I set the timer
for thirty minutes,
time to think it through.
The oven bakes a pie
for my brothers who grow up
in my kitchen doorway.
They grin at my apron.
To them I am a magician
pulling sweets from the air

The sounds of the house—

the telephone,
the timer ticking,
the creak of furniture
as my brothers slouch
waiting for the pie.
It is warm in the kitchen.
I freeze until the timer rings,
pour glasses of milk for my brothers.
No one should answer the telephone,
I tell them.

THIS MOTHER

This mother
darns herself into a sock,
hair smelling of molasses cookies.
She hadn't intended it
but finds it comfortable.
Blind in the new skin,
she slides from room to room,
discovers the house
for the first time.

This must be a plant, she muses,
snapping the stalk with her elbow,
and this a shoe,
flipping it over in the shuffle.
The stairway comes as a surprise
and down she bumps
toward the laundry room.

These new sensations
spur her on.
She ripples toward the dryer,
shimmies in,
her slamming shuts the door.
She tumbles, laughs, relaxes
in the warm and spinning air.
The threads are coming lose,
she thinks.

The buzzer sounds in minutes.
This mother ventures out,
head first.
Her body leaves the skin behind.

FAR FROM HOME

I inherited a skewed sense of direction from my mother, a baffling ineptitude on roads, in parking lots, in large buildings where the mind stutters, is paralyzed, and finally flounders its way home. Landmarks kept both of us mobile, as well as the kind stranger who translated east and west to right and left, who drew simple, friendly maps with arrows and *X* marking the spot.

I resented my mother's legacy—the helpless limbo I believed she'd bequeathed me—place of no-place I so often visited and laughed off after the difficult return.

This mutual deficiency has prepared me to understand the no-man's land my mother now has entered, her eighty-one years collapsed into a term someone called Alzheimer's. She has known this place all her life, and, like me, succeeded in finding her way out, until now, when landmarks have disappeared, and no words can be strung together to ask the way back.

All I can do is hold her hand, wander with her in the maze, and hope that my presence for her has something to do with home.

INHERITANCE

I remember your mouth
the broken wing of a bird
and the sighs you carried
in your pockets.
Your wrists and fingers,
twisted old carrots,
I can see them worrying
in your lap,
aching the old ache
we all had heard about.
Your back hunched when you walked.
As kids we stuffed rolled socks
under our shirts
and played you.
Now again, grandma, I play you.
The old ache, the sighs
visit me from your sleep.
I feel you working in my house,
I see your hands fumble with a jar,
I am awake to your sighs,
they are mine—
the sound of water as it passes
through pipes and gathers
to return to the river.

GRANDMOTHER'S RECIPES

I see it yawning on the counter,
its contents filed by those knotted fingers
that cradled my childhood face.
What she has in mind
for the table, the pantry, the cellar,
rests somewhere in this box of oak:
how to create a rising loaf,
transform a rind
into sweet translucence.

As she lifts a dog-eared card
the ceremony begins:
jars and canisters come forth
and mincing and sauteing
cloak me in their fragrant sound.

Her concentration is enough
to silence the house pets
and I, on the corner stool,
never ask to help her.

She performs alone,
and I play spectator to this day,
overseeing the recipes in her absence,
reading them without the time or skill
to do their bidding
and without her certainty
that what is held in a small oak box
will keep us all together and warm.

GRANDFATHER

I hardly knew the man,
though once I almost pulled a mole
right off his cheek
and kept it.
I was three or four.
What was he telling me
as I watched the mole
jump up and down?
Something about two blackbirds,
Jack and Jill,
Fly away Jack, fly away Jill,
come back Jack, come back Jill,
as he made bits of paper
disappear, reappear
between finger and thumb.
That is what I remember
of my grandfather.
Something about a face,
two blackbirds,
magic.

WHAT HAPPENS

My father is in Kansas
gently diapering my mother.
Her hands reach clumsily to help him
but only interfere.
Her mind has become nearly pure
as her heart.

This afternoon a fire alarm
interrupted my lecture
on William Carlos Williams.
In the parking lot
bright crushed leaves blew
and bunched around my students' feet.

Hours ago my husband
replaced my lost diamond.
We stared at its brilliance,
the many facets we could just
begin to name.

ASSURANCE

Not until after Mom died
did he have real things to say to me—
only daughter, perhaps his final confessor.
I think I listened like Mother—
half distracted, thinking about the disorder
of his bookcase, or what to make for dinner
while he quoted scripture
or tried to clear his throat.

Once his competent hands
took me to a place so deep
that nothing can describe its hold on me:
the way he opened a Bible, held an infant in baptism,
measured wood before he cut,
a steady certainty, as in a hymn,
its chords and promises
of blessed assurance.

When his infirmities
admitted questions and fears
into the rooms of his heart,
I could feel the shaking,
his clumsy efforts to hold on.
It was then I know I loved him best,
in the pale, imprecise light of final faith.

MEMORIAL DAY OREGON 2002

What to remember on this day
untouched so far by the past?
Here we are, perched on a mountain,
a bullfrog's low strum from the millpond,
my most tender brother
making our coffee, humming.
Late morning we hike the Lumberman's Road
with our father whose walking stick
sets our gravelly pace.
A sliver so thin it enters unfelt
and then the twinge, the shudder—
our mother gone,
her voice not even an echo.
Keeping the rhythm,
we are making our way to the spring
where water rises before us
in a gush like sorrow overflowing—
her face, her long arms around us,
herself now a mist in the distance,
ourselves beginning the return
back to our lives down the mountain
back to the place before this day began.

MINDING

She stops to collect stones and sticks
while he keeps his balance,
cane thumping over cracks,
morning easing into his bones.
When she runs ahead,
he calls to keep her near,
her brand-new shoes
barely touching the earth.

HIS DAYS

What is the last deprivation?
he wonders,
losing his wife,
her mind, then her body
still fresh on his heart.
He has fallen in the street,
the curb a step up
suddenly evaded him, leaving him
aware of the ranges of pain
deep in hip and arm.
Someone will come along;
he will learn to use a walker,
eat the food the institution
sets before him.

Some days float by
in a kind mist,
others grow thick with indignities,
rudeness, each patronizing voice.
He reads his Bible in fluorescent light
of the room he shares with a stranger
hoping the words still apply to him:
As for man his days are like grass,
he flourishes like a flower of the field;
the wind blows over it and it is gone,
and its place remembers it no more.
But . . . he has always loved that small word,
the one that turns everything around . . .
But from everlasting to everlasting
the Lord's love is with those who fear him,
and his righteousness with their children's children.

A basket of fruit arrives from his daughter,
a cheerful still life against the gray:
bananas embracing oranges,
apples rubbing shoulders with pears,
a world of cores and seeds and peelings
sweet as the one he is losing.

UNREST

From his nursing home bed
my father watches the news,
perplexed and stunned
by contradictions, the distance
between the Eisenhower he admired
and this cowboy, whose head,
a protest march balloon,
now floats across the screen.
The nurse brings in his medication,
pink and white blessings in a paper cup.

And then the onslaught begins.
Dixie and Alice, longtime residents,
take turns in their wheelchair assaults.
Propelling themselves down the hall
with demented, slippered heels,
they spot his lighted room,
and each in turn enters,
eyes flashing
with cryptic mutterings.
Alice grips his arm,
a shackle of bony knuckles;
he tries to negotiate, to humor her to leave.
Finally she does, and he returns to his biography
until Dixie wheels in
intent on tearing off his bedding.
The aides are busy in the west wing,
oblivious to these nightly sieges,
and when they are over,
my father, exhausted,
turns off his light
and dreams himself in a sane country,
treaties signed, sheets tucked in.

TALKING TO DAD FROM WEST OF IRELAND

Winds howl off the Atlantic;
our turf fire offers its limited comfort.
The connection is good
though his voice wavers like the flames.
He is letting go of this world
and I want him to hang on.
A new president, a new hope, Dad,
an FDR to fix it all.
I want him to believe we will be OK.
And from this vantage far away,
it seems a possibility.
Sheep graze in their slow way
high on the postcard hill
and the locals still weave their stories
face-to-face despite the Internet.
Something yet can happen, Dad,
a break in the clouds,
a full rainbow—one end of a mountain top,
the other in the lake below. And so,
in your nursing home room,
breathe some more days for me,
for you, for the clichés that sustain
our sure voices over the Atlantic.

MARRIAGE AND CHILDREN

here words weigh nothing
and all the players have won

THE QUICKENING

My dresses no longer hide
the size of me.
Stares at my belly
are more frequent, undisguised.
I buy milk and fruit,
read novels in the park,
gaze through branches
at cloud joining cloud.
Someone is living inside me,
I tell my friends.
They think I'm crazy.
This has happened since time began;
why the surprise?
But this is different.
No one has lived inside me before.
No one kicked or swam about
in my belly before this.
If you ask me, it's supernatural.
My husband laughs a lot these days.
He watches me
as I disappear around the corner
in the car or on my bicycle.
He waters the lawn too much
and picks the roses
before they are ready to bloom.

CONVERSION

I believed the summer
would end with his homecoming,
the windows grow opaque
in the house.
I would rock,
try to sing every song I knew.
I believed a tightness
would grow in my body
after the strain and pull
of his birth.
I would do what had to be done.

Instead,
he has caught me in his light.
He knows who I am,
a tree
bending toward its reflection
in the river.
There are times
I must look away
or go blind.

BAPTISM

The mother thinks of spinning
straw into gold,
all the secret names
she would need to discover.

The black wing of his robe unfolds
and for the hundredth time
he sprinkles water
on a downy head.

In this holy moment
the child cries,
fire and water
leap from the font.

Afterward people talk
of the fine white lace,
the tiny golden bracelet.
The minister vanishes into stained glass.

In the night the child cries out.
The mother gathers him up.
She rocks to believe he is safe.
She rocks to believe in the magic.

HELP

The zipper of a young boy's parka
is stuck midway
on a day turned warm.
The boy tries
to force it up or down,
then begins to worm his way
out of the thick, wooly skin.
He is mad
and his sneakers pummel the floor
as he pulls it as far as his armpits,
sways and hoots,
runs blind to his mother
who is folding a sheet.

She drops her work
and eases the coat down,
but he's madder than ever,
in a sweat, half-crying,
jerking away
from the hands he needs.
She works the metal,
smooths away the pinched lining.
Then he's loose.
With a spin, he flies outdoors.

She takes up the sheet
and sees her girlhood house
on the outskirts of town
by the highway.
She'd gather animals, half-dead
along the shoulder,
take them home to nurse.
Once in awhile
one would survive,
sniff her hand,
dash into the nearby field.

And the last white fold makes four—
animals whimpering,
bandages flying,
the field rampant with boys
running as far
as their thankless legs
will carry them.

OF MEN AND TROMBONES

My husband and son
are playing trombones.
This is something new.
Their big-boned bodies
strain forward on living room chairs,
their necks and faces
inflate and redden
like accelerated film footage
of ripening tomatoes.
They compete for volume and pitch,
a reckless fencing with blasts of sound.
To them, this is remarkable.
Each eruption is sustained
and slid about in the air—
a groan, a wail, a honk—
no music.
Sometimes they stop to laugh
the breathless laugh of athletes
gearing up for more sensational stunts.
The amazement of their own potential
overcomes them.
They have discovered
what the breath can do
when given a chance.
The neighbors' window blinds rise
in the hope of a finale.
As I make a move to say
it's time to stop, my voice slips and falls,
injures itself in the effort
to save the world
from the unleashed bellowings
of father and son.
Trombones held high,
they pass through layers of civilization,
ignoring the symphony, the parade,
the ragtime band,
blaring their way toward
some beautiful fraternal hell.

SON AT FIFTEEN

Music pours out
from under his door—
something with a message,
a promise, or a kick in the pants.
The fever of his youth
becomes the narrow shaft of light
his mother now expects and fears.
He grows away, his eyes avert,
he sprawls and shuffles,
belches, laughs in foreign octaves.
The milk he pours for breakfast
will be a balm to soothe his aches and hers,
to fill him full of whiteness.
But now his restless, furtive spirit
hovers in the hallway,
keeping her awake,
daring her to try to tuck him in.

MARCH 2003

Tonight my son unwraps thirty-two vessels he has thrown and glazed
and fired.

He sets them one by one on our table, eyeing them for flaws or
surprises.

He is the age of those young men now straining to see through a
sandstorm, trying to stay alive in a desert.

The bowls, mugs, and vases gleam with colors of the earth,
their pure forms comforting the room.

I imagine their rooms, like my son's, littered with CDs,
old skateboards, wacky posters, and signs,
renderings of superheroes, pop cans, books,
magazines, recruitment brochures.

Centering is the best part, he has told me.
You can feel the moment when your hands become still,
when the clay defies gravity.

Boys remain boys so much longer than they used to,
everyone keeps saying.
They live at home without a plan, work dead-end jobs,
grow restless, and drink too much.

These vessels will hold food, water, and flowers,
or simply fill an empty space with beauty.

One mother displays a framed photograph of her son,
his uniform, square jaw, and steady look
not far removed from the childhood face now breaking her heart.

I listen to the sound that pots will make fresh from the kiln,
a music like no other: *ping, ping*—
tiny chimes that play time's sad and ancient tune.

CROSSING THE BROOKLYN BRIDGE WITH OUR SON

It's July-humid, the New York City sky overcast
when we walk the bridge behind our son
who's holding hands with a beautiful woman.
From here you can see the East River
fashioned into waterfalls
by some hot artist
but we have eyes only for our son,
his long strides crossing
over an unbearable sadness,
leaving it behind
with the gulls,
those hapless hangers-on.

THE SCULPTOR

for Ron and Ben

Afternoon disappears
through a vent in the sidewalk.
A fruit stand breaks his pace—
a moment to look and fill a bag—
something more to carry.
Swings in the playground
slow as he passes.

Each day he has learned better ways
to carry more and more:
a bag of grapes, a boot buckle,
casters from a bed, a tail pipe,
part of a ladder.

He waits to light the room.
The pieces he carried from the street
cast shadows on the wall.
He sleeps facing them.

The light changes.
He stirs and wakens,
startled by these forms
so close to dreams.
He joins them piece to piece.
Nothing is more sure.

EXPECTATIONS

1.
You lived in a house
with a clean white table,
a cup of black tea,
the sound of pages turning
from all the living room chairs.

Your father was a minister.
You held your skirts
when you walked down stairs.
The Second Coming was scheduled
for 1948
the year you were born.

You watched your mother
flute the edge of a pie.
Her veins, close to the skin,
flashed blue
with each impression.
Her pies were always perfect.

In school you watched your teacher
fill the board
with good examples.
You thought they were so pure,
so white.

2.
At the corner mailbox
your letters fall
and mingle in the random pile.
You walk back home the long way.

You place buckets on the floor
to catch the drops.
Rain was not forecast
but comes in torrents
all afternoon.

A pear in your hand, half-eaten,
you watch the street
through the upstairs window.
Headlights glance the driveway
just as you turn to go.

You slide the silver combs
from your hair
and place them on the table
without a sound.
In the dark
you try to match your breathing
to his.

TO MY HUSBAND

The dog next door
keeps howling
the little deaf girl
on our block
keeps howling
leaves keep gathering
in wet parcels
under our tree
I am sick to death
of these warnings
nothing will come of them
I keep telling myself
it's only that I'm out of touch
with the sun
I swim
in the shadow of this house
breathing in splinters
and swallowing hard
I listen for the sounds
this is a dark time
stay in the clearing
and wait for me there

LISTENING TO SCRABBLE

My in-laws play Scrabble
at night with their son
while I read in the bedroom,
the door always ajar
like my book
half opened to sounds
of the game.
Small clicks of wood,
now a sigh,
my husband hums
(it's not his turn).
They ask each other,
Is n-u-x a word?
If I would watch
from the doorway,
two grey heads
and a peppered one,
bent low over troughs
of letters
would worry the tiles
eyes
dragging from letters
to board and back.
But I will not rise
from this nest of sound.
Here words weigh nothing
and all the players have won.

LUGGAGE

Someone lugs us out of the womb
and into the world—
and then our mothers lug us
in a pack or in their arms
to and fro—wherever they need to go.
Our fathers later lug us on their backs
or maybe out of bed for school.
And then we lug our books in backpacks
to our lockers, classes, home again.
We lug our duffels off to summer camp
and later lug our luggage out the door
and off to college.
After that we lug old furniture—couches,
book shelves, to our first apartments,
up flights of stairs
and down again too soon.
We marry.
Over the threshold groom lugs bride,
both lugging laundry to the laundromat.
And then we lug our own sweet children
into adulthood.
This lug-surey goes on and on
into old age
when what we do
is lug our aged bodies to and fro,
wherever we need to go—
stubborn, lumpy luggage
we hadn't expected—
these precious bags of skin and bones
not long ago lovingly lugged by Mom and Dad.
And finally all this lugging ends.
Released from baggage of this world,
no longer lugged or lugging,
we now are hugged and hugging
and floating in the heavenlies,
so light and luggage free.

THE UNUSED

Gathered over the years
a treasure of small things,
filling drawers, tins, boxes—
all sorts of strays, from pencil stubs
to single earrings and trinkets,
a tooth (was it mine?), a marble.
These are kept like forgotten secrets
as if losing one would hurt and scar.
The day I came across a Scrabble tile,
(M, 2 points) my mind unfolded
a very old message—
something about a promise I'd made
to my son who asked me if I'd make cupcakes
for his birthday party. *Of course!* I said.
I was terrible with frosting,
so I told him I bought some
decorated with little boats.
He said, *mmm* and then became very quiet.
That was thirty-six years ago.
The tile, those odds and ends,
each a reminder that nothing is lost
or useless—just hold one to the light
and let it show you where it belongs.

SPRING CLEANING

Once May was called spring cleaning time,
for taking up the rugs and scrubbing
walls and floors, for airing
anything that needed airing,
to rid the unclean world
of winter's airless sleep
and let the neighbors know about it.
Someone's mother's mother thought it up
imposing it on daughters
whose daughters finally put a stop to it.
Come June the windows will be closed,
the air conditioned,
nostalgia folded neatly into a paper fan.

THE SOUND OF MUSIC

So take me to a musical,
a tap-dancing, tear-jerking
baptism of bodies and bathos.
Give me spangles and corny lyrics—
There's a bright golden haze on the meadow
will do just fine.
However thin the plot,
the music will carry a sweetness,
a promise of reprise.
The meet-the-girl routine
never lets us down.
Back in real life, where my son's heart breaks
(he'd grown accustomed to her face)
and my mother has followed a yellow brick road
into another world,
I yearn for music to lift and swell,
for the ones I love,
to pick up the conductor's cue,
and in the spotlight's glow,
let sorrow become a simple song.

SMALL REMINDERS

He left the milk to sour.
It's up to her
to empty the carton
into the sink.
She traces a message
on the waxy cardboard:
This is the way with all whiteness.
This is the way with sheets,
bones, teeth, paper, carnations.
This is the way with socks
going about their business
behind my back.
They return,
not so white, empty,
skins discarded on the bedroom floor,
strange as the souring of milk.

Cups too hot to touch
steam between them
and much of what is said
rises also.
The kettle boils dry.
They didn't notice when it stopped singing,
when quiet in the kitchen
meant parch and ruin.

She counts the lines
on his forehead as he sleeps.
Some furrows go deep,
others can be smoothed away.
Some years were better
than others.
In this familiar place
lit by an off-white moon,
she counts and thinks of him.

IT IS JUNE

Daylight lingers into night,
grasses remain unparched, still tender and new,
the body rises refreshed,
the lawn chair is filled and relaxed,
trees shed their blossoms in the wind,
purpose breaks through clouds at sunset,
your touch has to do with my joy.
I will celebrate this month of light and promise.

CANDOR

Finally, your words emerge
from the sanctuaries
of your hearts. Shy but sure,
you confide in each other,
the space between you
breathing as one.

NEW YORK CHEESECAKE

The nonsense
you and I collected
over the years
creaks between us,
a clothesline of frozen laundry
with all its brittle gymnastics.
But this cheesecake, New York,
placed before us
at the right moment
grants us grace.
The smooth, rich song
of cheesecake renders us
eloquent, divine.
It melts into our throats
like some celestial cream,
then pumps through the arteries,
the veins,
settling gently behind the eyes.
We speak in the nuances
of lovers,
our words rising softly, freely,
like cheesecake
in the oven
oblivious to sneers of the subway,
the tired language of middle age—
rising above it all.

PARTING

So simple under water—
your body slides into the space
you open with your hands.
But on earth
the center is hard to find,
even with one eye closed.
Nothing holds still for the parting—
your restless child jerks away
from the comb,
your lover pulls the blanket from you
in the uneven hours of sleep.
Middle ground shifts
beneath your feet
and you fall on the side
you tried to avoid,
becoming your own shadow.

PLEASE TURN OVER

Repeated in a span of long married nights
a mantra so simple and clear,
there is no mistaking its intent.

Please turn over—
more declaration than request—
something a pet would understand.

We acknowledge one another's snores
taking turns at turning
between these sheets together
forty-some-odd-years,
like marshmallows in a campfire,
like well-greased gears.

BLANKET

This blanket isn't big enough
for us both.
We have torn the corners
to cover us.
Something in this room
has drilled our bed
into the floor.
Our feet are enemies.
We kick the air to find cover
and find only the icy skin
of each other.

If we could only wait 'til Easter
our skins would be enough.
We would be friends,
our nights would be easy.
This blanket would spread
to our growing
and fly with the winter birds.
We would be content
to lose this lovers' match.

QUESTIONS

Tell me something
is this what you wanted
a woman too tall
for the kitchen sink
who asks you more questions
than you can afford to answer
one who sulks by the heat vent
all winter
waiting
who prepares cups of tea
like ammunition against the day
always looking
for another kind more potent
chamomile for heartsickness
rose hips for aging
this is what I've come to
in my thirtieth year
what I need
is a new bike you say
and you buy me one
silver blue
with ten speeds
and turn that rare face of yours
to other things
I am sorry to blame you
no one else seems to be around
but on some days
when I hear the crocuses
trying to come up
I begin breaking out myself
I think of the warm mornings
when I am bursting
to tell you my dreams
the afternoons
you come in the back door
and I see you
just as you are
trying to guess
what lady will welcome you home

THE AGREEMENT

Here is a peaceable moment,
fleeting, easily rearranged.

The possibility
that I, you, she, or he
could find common ground
appeared a fiction with no alphabet.

In the heat of argument
words formed a chasm
deep and dangerous—
impassable.

Yet now we breathe
the sweetness of a treaty,
our willing bodies
given over to harmony and rhyme,
the letters forming our dissent
wrapping us whole.

STORIES

In the summer
we took turns.
One stayed with the children,
put away toys, read.
The other climbed to the roof.
The one up there
could hear the story—
golden hair cut and cast
from the tower window,
the gingerbread house of horrors,
the true one about three men
in a furnace.
From the roof
the chimney looked wide enough
for the wolf's descent,
neighbors wore patches
over one eye.
The witch wailed
It's only the wind,
and the drone lifting from the eaves
became silent.
When leaves scratched out
the last light,
the one on the roof
would climb down
glowing with fears
that put the children to sleep.

TO LOVE AND TO CHERISH

That face, that gesture—
a tenor of voice, a swish,
a nod, *I know what you mean.*
That hand, those opening/closing eyes,
the time of day or night.

The years, those children,
that exhaustion, that distance,
the hovering, the pride—
some sorrow, some loss,
a plate full, an empty nest.

A dinner, a daughter's wedding,
some rest, an award,
some wrinkles, a walk,
a holding, a leaning,
that face, that gesture,
that hand.

I SEE YOU, RON

I see you, Ron
in your orange, faded golf shirt
at the kitchen table.
You lean over a tablet,
adding Weight Watcher's points,
fervent as a scribe recording scripture.
Your salt & pepper hair
is sticking out in erratic tufts,
your huge, competent hands
carefully forming numbers.
You are thinking about
the glitch in your golf swing
that yesterday cost you on the course.
I see you
as I pad in my slippers
toward the coffee pot,
and I, like you, am counting . . .
all the numbers
adding up to love.

THE WAY I HEAR IT

The first burgers grilled this spring
anticipated like weekends
and sizzling under cover.
My husband hangs around the scene,
biding time with his tin whistle,
shooting an Irish jig, then an old hymn
into the green of May,
his broken ankle nearly mended,
his spirits rising like the temperatures.

Slick ice of winter, old hoodwinker,
the slipping, falling, breaking people
are finding their way back to rhythm.
They have learned the patience of bones
and stand at their grills
humming or tapping or trilling a tune
while petals fall like snow.

The waiting room tedium has ended,
the cast removed,
the burgers are done,
and my husband,
once again, makes music.

FATHERS AND DAUGHTERS

Fathers, look to your growing daughters,
their free and easy cell phone talk,
the way they linger in the doorway.
Look in their faces
for the woman replacing the child.
Allow the twinge of loss—
its strange unsettling nudge
to fine tune you for your task.

In you they see the well-lit future,
their home years unraveling swiftly now,
their lovers, husbands,
working their way
into your favorite sport coats,
into your very words.

On their wrists they will wear you,
in charm bracelets, birthstones,
watch your reflection glimmer on the wall
even as you turn away.

This is the time you are called upon
to speak the foreign language of your heart.

BRAIDS

Her hands separate
the strands of her daughter's hair
feeling in its texture
her own childhood summers—
the coolness on her neck
as she ran along the beach,
her braids striking the air.
Every day a grand expectation—
a leaf unfolding before her eyes,
its veins spreading in all directions.
At bedtime her mother released her braids,
brushed her hair
and praised its fullness,
its shining light.

When your mother braids your hair,
you must sit very still.
You will notice things you hadn't before—
a crack in the wall the shape of a teapot,
a scuff mark on your shoe,
the quiet breathing of your mother
as she weaves your hair
into countless indelible summers.

SEVENTH SPRING
for Madeline

New leaves peck their way
into the light,
their tender veins aching
for that surge of color.
All day winter clothes
climb attic stairs
and then sink into themselves.
Madeline holds a hairbrush
in midair.
She tilts her head
to watch the strange attraction.
Something draws a part of her away
like a new belief.
This is how her seventh spring begins:
leaf to light,
wool to darkness.
She starts to know
the longing of one season
for the next,
the sweetness of change
for its own sake.

WHEN YOU LOSE YOUR GLASSES IN SPRING

When you lose your glasses in spring
you feel little assurance
despite the smell of new air.
Delicate unfolding in the trees
and shoots projecting like hungry beaks
happen somewhere beyond the fuzzy realm
in which you sort anonymous laundry.
The twittering of sparrows
becomes a twaddering stridence;
puddles of sky in the alley
with their unmistakable gleam
and shifting scenery
are the only sure sign
that winter has melted
until your youthful daughter
walks in the front door,
her face a concerto you had forgotten:
Vivaldi's *Spring* crisp and clear,
her bright eyes seeing the melody for you.

BREAKING THROUGH

The girl yawns
and opens the blinds
to sober February light,
sees gouges in the snow—
marks of disfigurement and joy
where yesterday she plunged
through its heavy crust.

Last year the thick veneer
held her weight.
Her mother watched
the tentative skimming
of boots across the snow,
the weightless motion of arms
half suspended in air.
Rows of pines
spread their wide skirts,
shading the child's path.

When this year
the snow gave way,
the girl shouted and shattered
the crystal glaze.
Her boots kicked the shards,
sent them crashing
across the yard.
With her fists
she poked and punctured.
Clouds of breath
obscured her face
while her mother watched
from the window
this frenzy,
this breaking through.

DAUGHTER

From the window
I watch you and your friends
rocking the trailer, BUMP to one end
BUMP to the other—a gaggle of 12-year-olds
laughing down the petals from the plum tree,
waiting for my voice to scold, to stop your fun
and mouth the usual: *That will wreck your father's trailer.*
I've told you enough times before.
But my words will have to wait,
for I am watching how my daughter laughs,
her head tossed back, her hair splayed out like wings,
her mouth a nearly perfect O.
She grabs the elbow of her friend to keep from falling,
dizzy from the spell of laughter,
the world a blur of new spring leaves and sidewalks.
She is beautiful, I think, a little ashamed of myself
for such vanity—an indulgence
scorned by my mother and her mother before her.

I cannot disappoint them any longer.
Opening the front door is enough
to make the rocking stop;
the laughter turns to giggles.
I say my piece, and watch my daughter's face—
controlled, accepting, almost a woman's now
as she watches me turn
before the door closes softly behind me.

EIGHTH-GRADE VOLLEYBALL

The ball keeps hitting the floor
with a sickening thud,
and the one who said, *I got it*
drops her arms like useless baggage.
The coach is still spunky,
shouting stern encouragements
that skitter and slide across the floor.
This striving toward outsmarting
and out-muscling others
is not in their nature.
They say, *Excuse me,* ...
My fault, a hundred times a game.
I watch from the bleachers,
cheering for something fine and dear
in their politeness,
my own net drawn taut
between opposing teams
of what is learned and what is felt.

HERE WE ARE

Tonight I shop with my twenty-year-old daughter.
We trudge through the glitzy displays,
our attention fractured and dispersed
among the tiniest tee shirts and
worn-out jeans imaginable.
Gaggles of teenaged girls
stroll and pose, their bellies
peeking out, their eyes
darting wildly like hockey pucks.

What is my daughter thinking
as we turn onto the next blinding corridor,
window displays broadcasting
the sultry cleavage of youth?
I want to hold her hand
or whisper a prayer into her ear,
but instead, I try to keep up with her pace,
to brave the onslaught of techno music,
musky suggestions from the Body Shop.

When we return home, we both retreat
to our places of comfort.
Our purchases slouch in bags
by the stairway,
exhausted and forgotten.

SWEETIE PIE SONNET

for Madeline on her birthday

In you I see my girl child grown
To womanhood with grace and flair
Amazing how the time has flown
To this your nineteenth year.
When you were small, I knew the day
Would come when you would need
To break from me and find your way—
A truth that sometimes made me sad.
But on this birthday as I see
How strong and lovely you've become
I feel the letting go in me
Has drawn us closer than we'd ever been.
You're the sunshine in my sky,
My nineteen-year-old sweetie pie.

A BLESSING

A procession of Norwegian aunts
enters the living room,
walkers and canes setting a hectic rhythm
against the steady thrum of the coffee maker.
These are my husband's relatives—
the ones who outlived his father
and their other seven siblings,
the ones who scour us now
with their appraising eyes,
then settle on our teenage daughter
big boned and tall like them.
They haven't seen her in years,
and this visit, a kind of pilgrimage,
is weighted with our need
to see our daughter learn to swim
freely in her heritage—
an Ellis Island survival course,
a precollege encounter
with unschooled wisdom and grace.
Inga, Marie, Margit, Helen,
give our daughter your blessing
as she enters the world.
Give her your humor, your gooseberry jam,
give her your piecework, your hand-knit sweaters,
your long-living *yes*.
Give her a flag to hold,
a certain country in this uncertain world.

TWO

Something sweet as a mango
draws them together
in a city huge as heaven.
Neither owns the rights
to happiness, nor the key
to the heart's door.
Both stand on the threshold
between known
and foreign,
uneasy and smitten,
their faces in shadow.

LONGING AND LOSS

they cannot retrieve the music,
harmonies lost to thunder and storm

TONIGHT

Flames rumble in the turf
and wind plays the chimney
like a rusty flute.
The music says
something heavy to the heart,
something filled with stones
that will not stack
or children too big to carry.
Something holding back the tongue,
a weight that keeps the sitter
sitting in a chair
and promises no company.
This song that cannot lift itself
from minor key
has found an audience tonight.

FIVE COMPLAINTS

He is on the roof
shoveling snow
into my chimney.
He wants me to remember him
some way.

Bushel baskets
line the basement,
the back hall.
Sometimes I hear
skins bursting open;
too many tomatoes
and not enough neighbors.

I want to snatch
my children up,
swallow them back
inside my belly
away from the traffic,
the additives,
the naughty words.

The clothes hamper
bulges in the upstairs hallway.
Its wicker creaks with the sorting,
the washing, the drying,
the folding, the putting away.

Insulation seeps
through the cupboard cracks.
A gray dust
settles on every dish.
This morning
when I open the doors
I am sure years have passed
in my sleep.

THAT WINTER

What about the time
the trees were in ice?
People said they'd break off
if a strong enough wind
came along,
snap right at the joints.
I imagined yards full of treetops,
jagged rows of trunks
left headless.

But you assured me
the trees were strong enough
to take the blows
of any Minnesota storm
else why would they still
be around?

I told you
this is different.
It's like the time
I woke up and found
I couldn't make a fist.
My fingers were stiff.
I was angry
and I couldn't make a fist.
I expected it wouldn't last
but it did.

And the wind came,
snapped the trees right off
at the joints.
I could hear ice
shatter on our roof,
the squirrels in a panic.
You said we'd clean it up
in the morning.

MESSAGE

While you have been gone
I have worried about the icicles.
They gather like vultures
watching me come and go.
In the sun
they grow long and thin.
At dusk
shadows speak of their hunger.
This is a winter
to stay inside
where African violets
stay in bloom
and music drowns out the wind
where I can concentrate
on cups of tea and novels
about people who escaped
from Auschwitz or their husbands.
Where I can forget for a time
the cold intent of icicles.
I don't want to think
you sent them to watch me
but when you are gone
for so long in winter
the thought crosses my mind.

THREE GRACES

They've cloaked themselves
in winter
looking more and more
like the Fates,
their lucky sisters sitting calmly
spinning, measuring, snipping with shears
those foolish mortals' wasted years.

They are tired now,
and sobered by the way
things have gone.
Spring comes and goes
without much notice
and the zephyrs have too often
missed their cue.

Huddled and still,
they recall their dance
circling the centuries,
the scent of the blossoming world,
but they cannot retrieve the music
its harmonies lost to thunder and storm.

HUMMING

From a deep ravine in my heart
it will rise—a two-toned droning perhaps
the last vestiges of some
grief or sorrow—
startling me, but monotonous
as a murmur of treadmill going nowhere,
or the way my mother would stand
behind me as I'd sauté onions,
warning I would burn them or myself
before the hum has ended.
It will stun me in the midst of cooking,
dusting, washing dishes,
these vibrations and a tune's beginning—
the first notes on a broken clef:
muffled keening,
no one listening or joining me—
the single mourner—when grieving,
for all practical purposes,
has ended. Now and then I'll flinch,
fearing that someone hears the sound,
for they'll look askance,
and I'll clear my throat, swallow
this private song, muting it
with the beating of my heart.

WHAT IS HUMAN

Our cat, old, half blind
and crooked
knocks into things.
We keep him alive because
what is left of this sublime energy
we need to harvest somehow
and because
our children claim
he still has a quality life.
And what is this quality?
Maybe it's the extra petting,
the soft voices we use,
the expensive, mature cat food,
or our recent indulgence
in letting him shed
on any piece of furniture.
Eighteen years, he and his shadow
have patrolled our house,
modeling vigilance, lethargy,
and self-importance,
beautifying a ho-hum corner,
stepping into the middle of a book
or a conversation as if so say
there is nothing so strategic
as this moment—this time to curl or stretch
or purr—sensual as anything we humans can know.

MISLED

This is the wrong street.
She can no longer account
for the mistakes of her car.
Lately it has taken her
miles past her mark
as if to tell her
there is no point
to her business.
With each street
the wheels fatten,
pavement rolled
into black skeins,
the mystery
of her whereabouts
bound inside.
There is no unraveling.
She stops to ask a stranger
the way home.

THE LIMITS OF REPAIR

Where the pen stops mid loop,
where the groom hesitates,
where the gesture hangs limp,
where the cup spills its contents,
where the music grows strained,
where headlights freeze the deer,
where the father raises a fist,
where the nest lies empty on the ground,
where the voice falters,
then the father takes the pen,
the voice refills the cup,
the gesture shoos the deer,
the groom is moved by music,
and the nest?
There it lies, empty still.

EROSION

Everything is wearing thin.
The rugs, the dish towels,
our socks, this chair.
Look at it,
worn and soiled.
It's a crime
to let things go this far.
Nothing can be done
to bring them back.
Who can remember
when patches on jeans
were important?
My mother
turned collars on shirts
to make them new again
but that is over.
There is not time
to save things anymore.
I am afraid to bear a child
with this thinness all around—
sheets that tear when we toss in the night,
hair that falls
from our heads,
topsoil that washes
from our land.
Who can know
when these shoes will wear out
and my child will walk barefoot
over what is left?

DESERT

We are walking in a desert,
ageing far from home—
saguaros on the verge of flowering,
sand and scree crunching underfoot,
sky a gratuitous blue.

On the horizon something shimmers—
a possible quenching, but
it may be a golf cart, emblem of our kind
—someone seeking
a misguided orb in the tangle
of hunger and thirst.

WASTELAND

Desert basin floor
etched canvas of drought,
heat, and wind—
rains will come in time,
fill you up as if
plenty was expected,
as if the parched and starving world
could shrug off suffering
in the temporary mercy of the sky.
Reprieve, however it is given,
is a flower growing out of dust and stone.

ROOMS

Spare, metal hush,
place of no comfort,
retreat from company and light.
Rooms we live in, leave, re-enter
seeking safety . . .
door locked, heart caged.

REVISION

Revision is happening now as neighbors walk
their sturdy dogs to the park
and trees exhale their myriad of greens
along the boulevards.
I hear my voice speak words I didn't know I knew
and remember the clang of horseshoes hitting the spike
on family picnics when we were
who we thought we'd always be.

Disease spread its shadow
with such speed and deadliness
that no one had the chance to lock the door.
And now, as light returns and slowly
we re-enter the place we had to flee,
we feel a shyness.
We are bare and vulnerable
as newly shorn sheep
stripped of the life we believed we earned,
blinking in the newness of loss and gain.

ILLNESS

for Rosemary

Illness is a negative clipped to the wall.
Unsuspected, it shows up
in spite of everything.
Tenderness shuffles its feet at the back door
as Disbelief calls for a second opinion.
In the waiting room,
talk shows blare astonishing misfortune.
What could be worse than this?
Words from loved ones sound rehearsed,
the telephone is a broken arm.
While the body grows precarious,
the spirit gains a second wind
and gratitude settles into folds
of the hospital gown.
Now illness is a guest
to be treated with respect,
to be called by name.

LIMITS

The imagination offers its suggestions
as you watch your father's face
while he sleeps.
Its lines remind you of a relief map
of the Holy Land,
you want to think,
but instead you are simply
afraid he will die.
You pray for his mouth to close,
his breathing to even out.
This is no place for poetry—
for the controlled line
immune to sentiment
or to hysteria
sending you to and from
the nurses' station.
There is no art
in this raw territory
where the night shift
replenishes ice water
and your father
doesn't know your name.

MAKING FACES

Our mother now responds only
to funny faces—
those goony gestures of our childhood
that never failed to bring a laugh or snicker.
Her placid face, her nursing home posture
suddenly attend and brighten
to the gifts of sheer nonsense
offered by her middle-aged children.

My specialties
are the baboon and lizard faces,
favorites in my fifth grade class.
My fingers pull and push skin
to create the outrageous animal effect.
I work to make my mother see me
as all her children did and do again—
Watch me, Mom! we silently exclaim,
the urgency gripping us
like new orphans.

CHANGE OF SEASON

Perk up, your mother would say,
her hand lifting your chin
as if this gesture
could elevate your mood
or stop revelations about the world.
And for a moment her magic worked;
she knew your heart better than anyone.
To know and to be known, that is what you lose
as the middle of life
edges toward the margins,
as your husband falls ill,
as sleep, shallow and tentative,
threatens to abandon your nights,
as familiar trees become strange,
refusing to turn or allow their leaves to fall
even in the depths of November.
And now, your mother has nearly forgotten your name.
Her face still cheerful and full of light,
she thanks you for coming,
takes your hand, and says goodbye.

WHERE MOTHER WENT

She is not at home.
Her favorites have disappeared.
She is no longer the mother,
the wife, the violinist,
the maker of perfect pies.
Daylight through the curtains
she once made distracts her—
irritation, shadow birds.
The television she forbade her children
becomes her close companion—
the glitter, the laugh track, the gossip,
cheer her up in moments
between the dull pull
of trying to remember.
Her husband watches over her,
loves her even now
as she flutters with her hands,
as she moves into white light.

MOTHERS NEWLY GONE

Our mothers are leaving us.
One by one they flutter through the door
as if we had expected it,
as if we had prepared
for this good-bye.
We can hardly follow their recipes.
Their remedies for flu,
for heartache, are somewhere
in the cupboard;
the names of relatives to be invited
are mixed in with the old Green Stamps.
How can we, their busy daughters,
sew on patches to make things last?
What are we to do
with these old compacts,
these letters, cards, and cold creams?
How will we behave
without their disapproving frowns,
their *Listen, honey . . .*
their *Oh, sweetheart!*
We're standing up straight,
we're being kind,
and we've sent off the thank-you notes,
but they are minding other business
beyond the blue,
leaving us in middle age
to sift through their precious lives
for clues to who we are.

MORE LIGHT

From our porch we watch
the late June sky pale
in that space between sunset and night.
Days will shorten now,
fans of light closing
one by one,
a celestial tea ceremony
performed by all
the heavenly geishas.
This is the time
I feel least deserving of this life—
its cottonwood fluff, its blossoms,
its vacation photographs,
casual and relaxed as flip-flops.

Whatever prompts
subtraction of the light
will add the dark embroidery of dream
to heavy wool of winter nights.
Porch furniture stacked,
the cushions stored,
you and I will accommodate,
but not without another loss:
a child growing out of the house,
a parent, friend, or house pet gone.

In this solstice time
we feel eternal—
an effortless short-sleeved ease
in leafy greens and friendly barbecues.
We own a sweet forgetfulness
that leaves will fall,
that sun will age our skin,
and that this light is ours
so briefly on this uncommon earth.

DANCING

Once, I saw them
dancing in a hospital.
She had three weeks to live.
He had her in his arms,
her turban pressed against his chest,
her wasted body
following his lead.
Between them were no secrets,
no barriers now.
They danced so close
I could not tell
which body was dying.

SLEEP AND DREAMS

What will it take to fall
sweetly into the dark?

THE ADDING WE DO IN OUR SLEEP

The twirl of a gleaming baton
almost touches the rim of the dream.
When the march
takes a turn,
something else attracts the eye
lumbering deeper into sleep.
A bracelet winks
on the wrist of a woman,
the light of it blazes,
but you cannot look away
from the charms
reflecting a name
stitched in a cloth
framed on your grandmother's
bedroom wall,
some flowery name
that floats to the surface
washed clean of the thought
and the dream
and the sleep that held you.

RELEASE

Not in the drumming of rain
or the animal purr, the rustle of leaves.
Not in the crackle of fire,
in the jangle of bells, the lap of the waves.
Not in the skip of stone across water,
the flapping of wings
or the cricket's sweet saw.
But in the heavy human sigh,
arhythmic as dust—
surrender of breath to the open air—
the blessed letting go.

A WINTER'S NAP

In midafternoon, make your way
to your pillows and quilts,
tuck in,
dream of children
rough housing in the basement
while you iron the pages of a book
or follow a yellow spaniel.
The waking world can fret
as you travel so lightly—
snore through the troubles,
your sidewalk thickening with snow.

NO HURRY

All the urgent push and tug
under the rising sun, the setting moon,
have evaporated,
for now there is
nothing to prove or justify.
No one holds the reins
or spurs you on
as you slide through your day
without a shove.

ACCLIMATION

1. Water
She carries a fish bowl
wherever she goes.
She is the only one
who sees the fish inside.

She dreams in a shallow boat,
wakes to the swirl
and splash of water,
the leaping fish.

Her hands spread like starfish.
The sun rises
through the prism she holds.
This is the day the fish leaps from the bowl.

She thinks of places
to hide her young one—
in watery caves,
in skulls of men buried at sea.

2. Earth
She prepares tea
against the day—
chamomile for heartsickness,
rosehips for aging.

She drives the car to work
wishing it would float
and find a current strong enough
to take her back.

She holds a chambered shell
to her daughter's ear and knows
she too will bite the hook
knowing full well what it is.

She finds the heel
from her child's shoe
on the porch,
a footstep in such a hurry to go.

GOOD LITERATURE

The plot does not thicken,
but winds neatly around the heart
like a coil of clay
around the hand of the potter.
The action does not rise,
but folds, over and over itself,
waves on the Atlantic,
curling, vanishing, reborn.
The hospital scene
or the one on the dangerous river
are forever returning
as you drive to get groceries—
conversations between lovers
ring in your ears
like too much aspirin.
It will not go away,
this beautiful yarn, this winding
toward the inevitable, the necessary,
and the pages turn without you.
The final paragraphs you save
for those moments before sleep
when the reluctant eye
makes its way to the closing words
that curve and curl themselves around you
long after the book has left
your open hands.

HAUNTED

I can hear you
running bath water
in my sleep
you are on the roof
shoveling snow into the chimney
you want me to remember you
some way
you have forgotten
nothing is more vulnerable to the wind
than your footprints

HOTEL

She tries to settle in between the intervals,
forcing her mind to imagine waves
lapping on a summer shore
or fallen oak leaves rustling in the wind,
a steadiness that could summon sleep.
A wall away,
the sleeper makes primal music,
taking in and letting out the universe,
a thrum and crackle surging forth
with the confidence of only the unaware.
She begins to count each snore like sheep
and when she's reached an amazing figure,
she kicks away the quilt of pretending
and tries to match her breathing
to her neighbor's.
Tonight she will not sleep or read
or write or brood or watch TV
but concentrate on life and breath.
Keeping pace,
she finds a sort of sympathy
rising and falling in the antiseptic room
whose locked doors permit no strangers,
whose walls invite them in.

TENDING

Tending the pets of your adult children
stir in your uneasy sleep,
their needy snouts and soulful eyes
make you believe it is you who must
tend to them,
no matter if you are afraid

or have a life of your own.
Your children believe you adore their pets
because you have pretended,
fed them, walked them,
and petted them, their fur
dispersing itself over your life.

Every year your children ask you
what you want for your birthday,
and you hand them the same boring line
your own mother gave you:
Your Love is more than enough.
They interpret it broadly, and always send flowers.

When the petals drop, you sweep them
off the table, the final fragrance dissipates,
and you know you can never change
your odd ways of showing love.
Here is the bed you have made,
a bit rumpled, but all yours.

REST

The house is an asylum,
doors secured against invasion.
Nothing approaches, curious and shy
to distract the mind from its dark excursions.

The misery that awaits you
finds its way into your waking dream:
children late in returning,
the ego dealt a furious blow,
aging parents needing comfort,
the friend shaking his head in despair.

Your body shifts from side to side
seeking a hopeful wall to face.
Sirens and car alarms upstage the crickets.

Is there a place of rest,
some forest of cedar and sweet decay,
a soothing nocturnal world
of skittering paws and swoop of wings?

Can your body curl, your mind drift
on a bed of boughs
in the palm of God's hand?
Will that hand hold you up?
Will it heal wounds
grown large as continents?

THE MIND IS A STUBBORN ANIMAL

The mind is a stubborn animal
refusing the velvet offering of sleep.
The body, lion tamer in residence,
goes through the routine:
hoops and chairs and whips
and fancy footwork.
What will it take to fall
sweetly into the dark?
How will the mind succumb,
drop like a circus tent after
the wild applause?
Finally the three rings dissolve,
the body returns to its trailer,
the mind settles down
at the foot of the bed.

SIMULATION

An electric blanket
with its network of wires.
You cannot be sure
where the warmth
is coming from—
yourself, your lover,
those wires,
set at *2*
seems right.
The dial on the floor
has been taken
for a fish
an eye
a jewel
in the blear of dreams.

WHERE

Far from the station
from the slick of tracks and fluorescence.
Far from the brittle smiles
from speed, beep, and hum
from the soon-to-be-junked-brand-new.
Far from the nagging doubt
the empty chorus of not.
Close to the sweat of the earth
its granite bones a-shimmer.
Close to the flutter of wings,
the light-speckled forest floor.
Close to the swing on the porch
to the soundness of sleep
to the skin that is you.

WE ARE SLEEPING IN IRELAND

We are sleeping in Ireland
curled like the shape of the land.
The shush of the flue,
the rhythmic bleat of the lamb,
brush against our dreams.
This is the sleep of buried potatoes,
the sleep of fishermen
slack in the drift of the sea.
This is the sleep of the open hand,
of the mouth giving up desire
to the dark.

RE-ENTRY

Ireland, my deepest living sleep
I owe to your down-filled winter nights,
but each waking is a mortal effort
to confront your bone-chilling slates,
your verbal and liquid requirements.

Reasons to re-enter the wide awake world
seem few and thin when the unconscious
drifts in a green field, dense
in the rhythms of safety.

I need a cue, a rallying sign
to draw me from this tour bus of sleep:
someone rustling a cereal box,
kegs thumping from a delivery truck
outside the pub.

Back to sleep, then,
until the banshee of the Twelve Bens
hurls me from this bed,
points a crooked finger at my heart
and makes me swear to wide awake
in such a lucky land as this.

OUR DREAMS

Now we are telling each other our dreams,
piecing them together in stiff-bodied mornings.
A child or parent helps us find something;
we call the Humane Society;
a gingerbread man seeks a firearms license.
Coffee comforted, we make the kitchen table our stage,
with scenes more real than what we'll enter today
on the street, in the store, at Social Security headquarters.
The unfolding spectacle of our fear and desires
woven into this autumn sleep
have embellished our breakfast of eggs and toast—
lent it a sort of elegance. We are no longer required
to partake in the hurry of the past
and can linger over the hovering presences
feeding our sleep.
Sun peers through window blinds with tenderness
we believe we have earned, and we enter today
as if exempt from its exacting requirements.

NEW DAY

In the early hours of a Friday,
no sign of the black
hole of sleep or the snow of
forgetting under this starry quilt
my grandmother sewed by hand.
Returnable cans, towels
in the dryer, overripe bananas,
the regretful detective,
the film a dark comedy
I reluctantly direct, earplugs secured,
my pillows stacked,
while my dear husband,
in his museum of sleep,
keeps me company,
carrying me gently
toward morning light,
merciful in its constancy,
its buttered toast with real marmalade.

SECRET CAVE

From the corner of my eye
I see you watching me.
You pretend you are asleep,
black beard folded into sheets,
one paw curled
around your shoulder
as if you are cold
or modest.
I bend to find my shoe
near enough to the bed
to assure myself
of your attention.
For years you spy on me
before the sun,
steal a look
then quickly close your eyes,
a great bear blinking,
watching me love you
from your secret cave.

HOPE

Bless whatever music plays
in these precarious, precious days.

THE QUALITY OF MERCY

Her work is wasted, they say,
as she tries to lift the weight of sorrow
heavy as a brickyard
or a prison gate.

What can Mercy do
beneath this empty sky
with her few blankets,
her dwindling source of water?

How can she turn her solemn face
to Misery again and again
collecting his tears,
hearing him ask to die?

Come, she says,
*I will do what I can
and when I leave you,
mark the place where I knelt
beside you with a stone
too heavy to cast at your brother.*

TROUBLES

They are stones
deep within you.
Light and heavy
they rest, unstirred
for perhaps years
before event, the accident,
the loss of what you know
and love.

Some will be unfazed
by the tumult,
will remain in the fixed
design of your uniqueness.

Others will roil and churn
through your days and nights
of endurance
until somehow,
a settling, a reprieve,
a forgetting or forgiving.

MENDING

Not in the seam, simple to repair,
but torn in the fiber and weave of it.
How to piece together such damage?
Some miracle of spirit,
thread to thread to thread,
the patient work
laid out here, before us.

HOLDING BREATH

How long can you hold your breath?
I'll time you.
When you think you have reached your limit,
count to ten.
Your lungs are stronger than you think.
They have taken in the anger of your house
and held it like a lover,
for years retained your envy,
nearly turned to tissue now.
I'll count and then you count
and finally when your face is crimson,
and all your will is spent,
allow your grievances to crash into the world—
unhoused, exposed, ridiculous.

GARBAGE TRUCKS IN OCTOBER LIGHT

Squirrels are ruining the pumpkins
and neighbors have raked leaves
into our driveway. The same dog
behind the fence keeps up a high-pitched bark,
blight has finished off the ash trees,
summer produce lies spoiled in the refrigerator.
And here comes the garbage truck.

October light falls over the damaged world:
all is equal to the red and gold.
The bluest, blinding heavens spill fire
over us and what we know, as if to say,
rake up your grievances,
burn them now before the freeze of winter
locks them in your heart.

HOLD YOUR HORSES

for Lambert

Lasso truth
like a runaway steer
and you will find its veins
running cold.

Approach it like a lover
with a ribbon for her hair
and truth, in time,
will lean in your direction.

A CHOICE

So little light is needed
to learn the height and depth
of space you inhabit.
You can make the walls echo
with the measure of your voice,
and somehow be content
with slivers of truth and dim confinement.
Or,
summoning all your senses
build a scaffold of desire;
climb up and out
of this empty drum
into a sunscape, vast and alert.

ALLOTMENT

We are given the gift of days
each wrapped in promise,
luster, and mystery.
Boredom is the odd man out,
granted a corner to sit
and twiddle his ungrateful thumbs.

HARD WORK

What your great-grandfather did
with his hands should interest you
as you look at your own,
dexterous beyond imagination.
Fingers calloused and stiff,
he pulled stones from his land
and stacked them like old grievances
to mark the boundaries.
He grappled with the earth
until his hands curled,
the handle of shovel or rake
defining his final infirmity.

Your occupation, you say,
demands nothing of this sort—
the switch and the keyboard,
hobby and sport—
but look at your knuckles,
your capable palms—
What can they do
to make something last?

INSTINCT

What makes the young man
defy the tank in Tiananmen Square,
the fireman enters the flaming tower,
the mother wraps her children with her body
when machine guns rain their fire?
Will the fox preserve his species,
the chameleon turn convenient colors
to be taken for a leaf or branch?
This does not diminish
what we as humans do
but instinct keeps up her uncanny fight
after the flesh and spirit flag.
She's ready as the wind
to give us a surprising push
into the fray of human disaster,
to flex the unused muscle of our will.
Such a gift for those of us
whose courage falters,
whose hope for our survival rests
on strictly what we're made of.

WHEN THE HAND LOSES ITS MUSIC

When the hand loses its music
the instruments gather dust.
Your child turns his back
on the finger that beckons and scolds,
on the hand that quits becoming
the rock or the scissors.
Your lover misses your caress,
the neighbor your salute.
The two of them join hands.
Your ruined fist
gapes like an empty purse.
Even your outstretched hand
is misread
as a signal to stop everything.

When the hand is mute,
the heart must speak for it,
perform sleight-of-heart tricks.
The heart tells more than a gesture.
It makes a bold resound,
defies infirmity.
The hand can go, enter a monastery,
while the heart cracks its knuckles,
plays the entire concerto with variations,
drums you back to your old command.

HER HEART

It is an error to call her heart
only a precious mitten of feeling,
kindness, or containment.
Her heart is also the limping ice man
calling out in the pale morning.
Sometimes her heart bucks and kicks
in its meager stall,
a space too small for its thumping desire.
Call her heart an ornamental flower,
an old shoe, a beloved uncle,
and she will beat you out of her system.

MARCH

Today my high school band marches
across my memory, winding back to the '60s,
a parade of shimmering drums and horns,
synchronized steps to a steady beat
soon repeating its throb in boot camps,
protests, the sound of choppers
hovering over Saigon.

Main Street has altered like those fresh faces,
eyes fixed on the drum major, a skinny boy,
whose power to set the pace couldn't last
beyond football season.

Watch it disappear around the corner—
the marching band—
heavy on the bass,
following whoever wields the baton
fifty years into the future
in 4/4 time. Nothing can stop its pulse,
its misdirection, its efforts to find the way home.

HUMAN

Something moves
alert under this sky
earmarked for survival.
It talks and walks,
remembers—
making its way across the planet,
taking ownership.
It eats and sleeps,
desires.
There is not enough
to fill it
or calm it.
It thinks and hurts,
imagines.
No grave can hold it—
this skin and bone and beating heart.

ALL I EVER WANTED

To step out of this suit of armor
crab from shell,
insect from chrysalis,
a new creature
composed of antennae and necessity.

PRACTICES OF THE HAND

The doctor
takes her hands in his.
He knows the names of the tiniest bones,
the most elusive tendons.
He knows the full range
of the hand's motion,
the possibilities of the hand.
The hand is a miracle,
he says.
All the intricate workings
to lift one finger—
like a little factory
operating under the skin.
He moves her stubborn fingers
as he talks,
makes notes on them.
She hopes he can fix her hands,
make them work again,
take hold of her children,
her china,
before she loses them.
She watches the hand
of the doctor as he writes.
It moves with precision
filling the page.
Her hands drift to her lap.
She can buy new hands
she is told.
She can forget the nights
she wakes,
her hands turning against her,
the days she keeps them buried
in her pockets.

She kneels in the garden
pulling weeds,
fascinated by the movement
of her hands.
Roots grip the soil
but she pulls with all her might
and not one weed survives.
She will use these hands
against the earth's imperfections.

KEEP IT UP YOUR SLEEVE

Why not spill and spell out
all your thoughts and imaginings,
your diet, your views, your vanities?
Someone will take note of your remarkable life,
spin it like a tale, tall and memorable.
Instead tell no one.
Enter the realm of your true self,
private space of wonder, arena of soul searching,
a garden surrounded by hedges and bittersweet.

WHAT BLOOMS

An outrageous gaggle of peonies
lean their luscious shoulders
against the neighboring barberry,
unaffected by its barbs,
its dangerous indifference.
Ants explore their silky petals,
teeming magenta,
their voluptuous folds—labyrinths of delight.
The luxury of such blooming,
its splash and dazzle
awakening the woman
whose birthday has just passed.
Here is a way to live, she thinks,
to make a fiery show, fade then fall
in the grace of the season.
The eye of the sun
films this progression:
her beautiful life pushing up
from the earth with such green might,
budding in the days of marches, revolutions,
blooming in the loves she found, that found her.
Her now-muted colors against the trellis of her years
strike her in the strength of the moment.
She feels her spirit twining upward,
greedy and grateful
for the remaining light.

GETTING WELL

The sound of shovel on concrete
carries down the block.
Crystals light on the metal backbone,
a yearly custom,
chasing the first snow
as it falls,
training it early
away from foot paths.
Better to let it be
a time to build and lean
against a snowman,
to place the coals of his eyes
over your own,
to breathe deep
into the drowsy spirals
and let the neighbors on either side
cut perfect paths
leading nowhere.

I REMEMBER FLOATING

I remember floating
lying on the water
my body allowing
its small downward pull
until a flutter of my arms
and feet steadied me.
Come swim! I heard them call
from somewhere
but I was elsewhere,
a dreamy girl watching
the heavens
through closed eyelids
oblivious and out of range,
disillusionment yet to find its way
into my heart or illnesses into my body.
I trusted water to keep me afloat
like the hands of my mother
who made me believe, as I do now,
that buoyancy lives in me
and in all of us no matter
how far we are from shore.

NERVE

Daredevils count on blood cells
to repair their disrespect
for gravity and mothers' fears.
No damage too great,
no trauma too fierce
can still a heart
so set on hazard.

Give me some of that
to fuel my final years,
to foil the safe, appropriate
me, the one who always looked both ways,
and then again—
or didn't look
temptation in its gorgeous eye.

Sometimes, before I fall asleep,
I tread the water right before the falls
and then let go—
not death, exactly,
but the rush of entering the danger zone,
my blue pajamas swirling.

RECKONING THE WATER

The one who walks by water
risks more than drowning.
As sun ignites trees
on the far shore
gulls and whitecaps flashing,
he loses his footing
in this world.
Clouds proceed
solemn and sure of their way
as the fish beneath.
His eyes are drawn
along the shore
resting on a dune,
a sweep of pines,
the sun splintering red
in the west.
Now he knows the longing
of Moses or Gatsby—
some sign or light across the water,
some current strong enough
to take him back
to what he once knew so well.

LUCKY YOU

Sure enough, you got the job,
won the lady, found your place
on the planet earth.
Don't sit there smiling
like the Buddha.
Shine your light, golden boy.
Turn good fortune into water,
water into health.
Thank the rabbit for its foot,
the horse for his shoe,
and bow your head under the lucky stars.

FATHOM

The rare times
I have joined hands with despair,
I somehow knew I could let go,
back away, return to my place at the table.

The hurting ones circle all around us,
a ring of ragged cut-outs
at home with nowhere.

At night when sleep remains the thinnest veil,
I feel the guilty surge of gratitude
sweeping me back to a congregation
of children yet-to-be born,
all hands raised to be chosen
for a life like mine.

SHRINE

Touch it, bend it, drop it,
let it weather in all seasons—
it will remain steadfast.
The dependable heft
creates in us a longing
in this cyberworld
replete with flimsy promises
and disguise.
Give me a solid piece of earth,
a steely hunk of matter,
and I will make a shrine
to honor and live by.

KINDS OF DAYS

There are those
that wrap themselves
around your legs like small children.
All your attention gets mixed in a bowl.
The telephone rings and rings.
You count the talking plastic holes.
When you finally make a move,
it is in place.
The rug is worn
where you have spent these days.

There are those
clean and sharp as a blade of grass.
Intentions slice neatly into the hours,
the book is completed, the weeding is done.
The fish bites the hook, you swallow no bones.

Then there are those
when you win the grand prize.
The red dress finally fits.
An old lover appears at the door
with orchids.
Under the bed
you find the long lost key
and at night the pillow cracks
with the weight of your dreams.

PUMPING
for Pamela

We are priming the pump,
taking turns at the age-old exertion,
and we laugh at the inept
ways of our arms and hands,
unused to such homemade rhythm,
such resistance to our needs.
The metal handle shrieks with each motion,
cries out in lament for all women
whose priming brought no water,
who never felt the gush of plenty
no matter how hard the pumping
exhausted muscle and bone.

We who have spent our tap water lives
exempt from the labor of great-grandmothers
have this day discovered the beauty of pumping,
of our powers to draw water straight from the earth.

Humbled and hopeful,
we watch as the clear stream splashes,
each offering a single gift:
this one for healthy childbirth,
another for free-flowing tears,
the next for cleansing, and then for nourishing,
and on and on until the bucket is filled with blessing.

CREAM

Here
skimmed off the top
a moment on the lips
the tongue
swallowed
rich in the throat
cream in the stomach
cream pumping in the veins
swirling in the head
thick and cold
behind the eyes

THIS IS MINE

How many shopping carts have I usurped
and pushed toward the dairy section,
more Swiss needed for sandwiches,
before arrested by a cartless stranger
re-claiming his own groceries, my apologies
spread thick on those fluorescent afternoons,
a reckoning stretching back to the flickering fire
of my first recognition of *this is mine,*
a toddler's declaration that a baby doll
in the toy basket belongs in her arms only?
But Mother forming another meat loaf,
hands greasy, apron smeared,
gives me a look, stamped like the Old Testament
upon my forehead: *nothing belongs to you only.*

As I loosen my grip, my children, my house,
my good intentions, all are claimed by others;
even my story, the one I live right up until now,
begins to drift from my care before
I learn again the good news: that I am
released from all I thought was mine.

THE COMMON WONDERFUL

Your aging face has now become
beautiful to you—riverbeds
and softening earth, seasons
of droughts and rain.
You see your reflection
in this sequestered place,
and say *yes.*

Silence falls between words as if
an endless game of Scrabble
between you and God
replaces the seething news
savaging your days and nights.

The Old Master's painting, restored
from dim to bright, layers of time
removed, and what was thought to be
a boulder becomes an elderly man,
walking with a child.

In the slow motion of this present world,
a freight train rumbles cross the town,
guided and held by tracks laid
long ago in the heyday of progress.
It travels with confidence, forward,
to a place in need of its cargo.

AFTER

Some make the passage with ease,
but you and I, our feet unsure,
inch forward.
In our element,
we see the earth up close:
elders with no time to lose.
Ears to the ground,
we learn what comes next.

BLESS THE DAYS

Bless the days that linger
in our laps like contented pets.
Bless those that topple
down like children's blocks
and make us grateful even for regrets
when we look back
at our misguided tracks.
Bless whatever music plays
in these precarious, precious days.

ALL FINE IN THE FLOATING WORLD

No signs of turbulence—
day spills into night,
peninsulas shift and shed
islands in slow gestation.
A current gently breathes
the next departure,
the next merging.

WHAT IS OUR DEEPEST DESIRE?

To be held this way in our mother's arms,
to be nestled deep in the warmth
of her body, her gaze,
to be adored, to overwhelm her
with our sweetness.
This is what we seek in chocolate,
in the food and drink and drugs
that stun the senses, that fill the veins
with the rich cream of well-being.
What we take for lust—can it be, perhaps,
a heavy pang of longing to be swaddled
close, close to the heartbeat of our mother?
No bucket seats, Jacuzzi, or even a lover's embrace
can duplicate this luxuriance,
this centered place on the roiling planet.

When the old woman now small and light,
can be carried in the arms of her son,
he, at first, holds her tentatively,
a foreign doll,
but gradually, as the pool loses its ripples,
he sees his face in hers
and draws her to him,
rocking to the rhythm of her breathing.
This is the way to enter and leave the world.

Miriam Pederson (1948—2023), poet, professor, mentor, and loving wife and mother, grew up in Minnesota and Illinois as a pastor's daughter. She understood her calling as a writer early on, as expressed in her eighth-grade autobiography *A Rose Among Four Thorns,* in reference to her four beloved brothers. She taught high school English classes for six years in Minneapolis and St. Paul, Minnesota, before moving with her husband, sculptor Ron Pederson, to Grand Rapids, Michigan, in 1977.

In Grand Rapids, Miriam immediately became active in the poetry community while teaching middle school and high school English. While attending Western Michigan University as a graduate student in creative writing, she served as resident poet-in-the-schools for twenty-three West Michigan and Upper Peninsula schools funded primarily through the Michigan Council for the Arts. She also began her career as an adjunct professor of English and Creative Writing in three area colleges including Aquinas College.

Upon completion of her MFA degree in Creative Writing at WMU in 1984, Miriam began her twenty-nine-year career at Aquinas, where she taught English literature, creative writing, and humanities and began the creative writing program. She was a frequent lecturer, workshop leader, and presenter for elementary, secondary, and undergraduate students, for retirees in the Osher Lifetime Learning Institute at Aquinas College, and for poetry groups in Ireland, where she spent five semesters leading Aquinas College's Ireland Program with Ron, who was also a professor of art at Aquinas.

An ardent advocate of the arts and humanities, Miriam served on the board of the Urban Institute for Contemporary Art and started its creative writing program, serving for eight years as its project director. She also served as board member of the Grand Rapids Area Council for the Humanities for six years, including one year as director, during which she initiated the Poet Laureate of Grand Rapids project and nominated the first two Poet Laureates of Grand Rapids. She also won the Kent County Dyer-Ives Poetry Competition and served as its manager for one year.

Miriam's poetry has been published in her chapbook, *This Brief Light* (Finishing Line Press, 2003) and in thirty-seven anthologies, journals, and small press magazines including *New Poems from the Third Coast: Contemporary Michigan Poetry*, *The MacGuffin*, *Passages North*, *The Book of Birth Poetry*, *Christianity and Literature*, *Sing Heavenly Muse*, and *Song of the Owastanong: Grand Rapids Poetry in the 21st Century*.

For thirty years, she worked with her husband Ron in creating collaborative poetry and sculpture exhibitions. In the last decades of her life, Miriam regarded this collaborative work as the equivalent of publishing. Together, Ron and Miriam completed fifteen collaborative projects which resulted in eighteen exhibitions of poetry broadsides and sculpture. Miriam's poems in collaboration with Ron's sculpture have been exhibited in Grand Rapids and regional galleries and are documented in three collections of images and poems: *The Adding We Do in Our Sleep*, *Doubletake*, and *Evidence of Things Unseen*. Miriam and Ron were married for nearly fifty-two years.

While reflecting her experiences, Miriam's poetry especially highlights her love of family and her extended "family" of many friends. To the very end of her life, she was more concerned about her family and her friends than about herself.

POSTLUDE

I WISH YOU THIS JOY

Joy, sneaking up, unsuspected, under your tablecloth,
out of the pages of your book,
falling into your lap from a neighbor's tree.
Joy, alerting you to smells of sawdust, frying bacon,
to pines and superglue, mown grass and Juicyfruit—
the same joy of the belly laugh, of the well-played tune.
Joy, dispensing sweet petals of grace in the hospital room,
in the back seat of your car as you drive to work.
Joy, snapping you out of yourself and into your rightful place—
for moments that sustain and bless,
I wish you this joy.

www.ingramcontent.com/pod-product-compliance
Lightning Source LLC
Chambersburg PA
CBHW071713140626
46557CB00011B/13